www.ingramcontent.com/pod-product-compliance
Lightning Source LLC
Chambersburg PA
CBHW071900090426
42811CB00004B/684

Geomancy

Unlocking the Magic of Earth Divination for Beginners

Your Free Gift (only available for a limited time)

Thanks for getting this book! If you want to learn more about various spirituality topics, then join Mari Silva's community and get a free guided meditation MP3 for awakening your third eye. This guided meditation mp3 is designed to open and strengthen ones third eye so you can experience a higher state of consciousness. Simply visit the link below the image to get started.

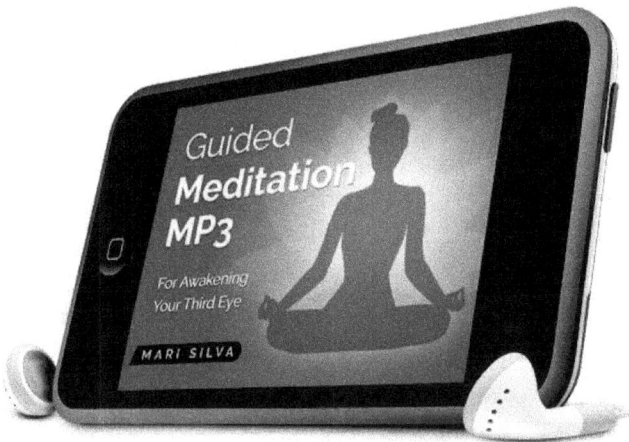

https://spiritualityspot.com/meditation

Table of Contents

Introduction

"The five elements are energies, not things. In Hinduism, they are known as the five tattvas. Psychic people can see them and their geometric forms."

~~Stefan Emunds

Have you ever wondered what your future holds? Have you ever looked up at the stars and felt a deep connection to the cosmos? If so, you may be interested in learning about geomancy.

Geomancy is an ancient form of divination that uses the power of the earth to answer your questions. It is a form of earth magic that can be used to gain insight into your past, present, and future. The word "geomancy" comes from the Greek words geo (earth) and manteia (divination). The word "geomancy" can also be used to refer to the study of the earth's energy field.

Geomancy has been around for centuries and is still used today. There is no perfect way to do it because each practitioner has their techniques and preferences. However, the basic premise is that we can gain insights into our lives and the future by using the natural world as a mirror. This guide will teach you the basics of geomancy, including how to cast your geomantic chart.

In the first chapter, we will explore the history and origins of geomancy. We will also discuss the elements that form the basis of this practice. In the second chapter, we will discuss why planets matter in geomancy. We will look at the zodiac signs in the third

chapter and how they connect to the elements. The fourth chapter will focus on the geomantic houses and their meanings.

In the fifth chapter, we will discuss how to prepare your mind for a geomantic reading. The sixth chapter will teach you how to cast geomantic points. The seventh chapter will focus on the different geomantic figures and their meanings. We will show you how to construct a shield chart in the eighth chapter. The ninth chapter will focus on generating an astrological chart. Finally, in the tenth chapter, we will discuss different methods of interpretation.

You will also find a bonus section with printables to help you start your geomancy practice. With the help of this easy-to-understand guide, you will be able to tap into the power of the earth and use it to gain insights into your life and your future. So, regardless of whether you are a beginner or an experienced practitioner, this guide will provide you with everything you need to know about geomancy. So, let us get started!

Chapter 1: Introduction to Geomancy

Are you looking for a way to understand yourself and your place in the universe? Do you want to know what your destiny holds? Geomancy can help you get answers to these questions and more.

Geomancy is rooted in nature.
https://pixabay.com/es/photos/avenida-%c3%a1rboles-sendero-815297/

Many considered a divination system as old as time; geomancy was once practiced by cultures all around the world. This system of divination implied direct contact with the earth, the spirit realm, and

astrological alignments. In this chapter, we will look at geomancy's interesting cultural and historical background. We will also explore how to practice this ancient type of divination.

Geomancy - The Divination System

Geomancy is a divination system that uses the earth to understand the hidden forces at work in our lives. Also known as "earth magic," geomancy is rooted in the belief that the land is alive and has wisdom to share with us. The word "geomancy" comes from the Greek geo (earth) and manteia (divination).

To practice geomancy, one simply needs to spend time in nature and attune oneself to the earth's subtle energies. The shapes and patterns of the land can then be interpreted as clues to our highest potential and deepest desires. By connecting with the earth through geomancy, we can access our hidden power and learn to live in harmony with the natural world.

A Brief History

Geomancy is an ancient practice that has its roots in the shamanic traditions of Africa, Asia, and the Americas. It is also one of the oldest forms of divination in Europe, where the Celts and other indigenous peoples used it.

Geomancy uses the placement of objects to interpret the will of the universe. The word "geomancy" comes from the Greek word for earth, and it is thought that the first geomancers were likely priests or shamans who used rocks, sticks, and dirt to divine the future.

The first written record of geomancy comes from ancient India, where it was known as "Vastu Shastra." This Hindu text describes the use of geomancy to find the perfect location for a home or temple. In China, geomancy was known as "Feng Shui," and it was used to align buildings and burial sites with the flow of "chi," or life force energy.

In Europe, Geomancy was used by the Celts and other indigenous peoples to find sacred sites for their tribes. The Druids, in particular, were known for their skill in reading the land. They would often travel to far-flung places in search of special places to

build their temples and altars.

During the Middle Ages, geomancy was popular among both Christians and Muslims. It was also used by the Knights Templar, who were said to have used geomantic symbols in their magical rituals. The Renaissance saw a revival of interest in geomancy, as many scholars began to rediscover the ancient texts that described this divination system.

Over time, the practice of Geomancy spread to other cultures, and different methods of divination developed. In Europe, for example, geomancers began using bags of sand or dirt to create patterns that could be interpreted. Today, there are many different schools of geomancy, each with its methods and traditions. Although some people may view it as a superstitious practice, geomancy has been used for centuries to help people make important decisions about their lives.

Cultural Relevance

Geomancy has played an important role in many cultures around the world. In Africa, it is still used by traditional healers and shamans to diagnose and treat illness. In Asia, it is used to select auspicious locations for homes and businesses. And in the Americas, Native American tribes have used geomancy for everything from choosing hunting grounds to predicting the future.

Although it is not as well-known as other divination systems like tarot reading or astrology, geomancy is still practiced by people all over the world. And with its simple techniques and earth-based approach, geomancy is a great way to connect with the natural world and access our hidden power.

Geomancy is a very practical method of finding answers to specific questions. It involves interpreting patterns in the earth to gain insight into a particular issue, for example, the placement of rocks or the shape of a mountain. This might seem like an arcane or outdated practice, but it is quite useful in modern times. For example, geomancers have been used to help locate natural resources, assess environmental impact, and predict natural disasters.

In addition, the principles of geomancy can be applied to more everyday matters, such as choosing a location for a new home or business. Whether you are looking for answers on a global or personal scale, geomancy is worth considering. The next time you have a question, why not ask the earth?

The Practice of Geomancy

Traditionally, geomancers would use sticks, stones, or other objects to create patterns in the dirt. These patterns would then be interpreted according to a set of rules to divine information about the future or answer specific questions. Although the practice of geomancy has largely been forgotten in the modern world, it remains an interesting way to engage with the natural world and gain insight into the hidden forces at play in our lives.

Geomancy is a simple and accessible way to connect with the earth and receive guidance from the natural world. All you need is a piece of paper, a pencil, or a bag of sand or dirt. To begin, you will need to clear your mind and focus on your question. Once you are ready, start making marks on the paper or in the sand. There is no right or wrong way to do this, just allow your hand to move freely.

After making a few marks, take a step back and examine the patterns you have made. See if you can find any shapes or symbols that seem to stand out. Once you have found a few potential symbols, look up their meanings in a geomancy guidebook or online. With a little practice, the accuracy of your readings may surprise you!

The Different Types of Geomancy

There are several different types of geomancy, but they all use the same basic principles, the belief that everything on Earth is connected to the universe above it and that everything has its unique energy pattern. Astrologers have long believed that each planet influences a specific part of our lives and personalities. Therefore, they believe that by studying these patterns, they can predict events or outcomes in your life.

Elemental Geomancy

The most common type of geomancy is called elemental geomancy. Simply put, it is the practice of using the elements of earth, air, fire, and water to create harmony in our lives. This may sound like a new age concept, but the truth is that people have been using these principles for centuries. For example, Feng Shui is a form of elemental geomancy that has been used in China for millennia. The basic idea is that by aligning our environment with the natural flow of energy, we can create balance and harmony in our lives.

There are many different ways to practice elemental geomancy. One popular method is to use crystals and stones to create an energetically balanced space. Placing these stones in specific areas can help redirect energy flow and create a more positive environment. Another way to harness the power of the elements is through meditation and visualization. We can access their wisdom and guidance by connecting with the elementals, the spirits of earth, air, fire, and water.

The method also involves interpreting patterns made by dividing a map into four quadrants, each representing one of the four elements, air, fire, water, and earth. There are many different methods of dividing up the map and reading the results, but all involve finding a balance between opposing elements within each quadrant.

Whether you want to create more balance in your life or simply connect with nature on a deeper level, elemental geomancy may be worth exploring. You may be surprised at how helpful and accurate this ancient practice can be with a little practice.

Astrological Geomancy

Astrological Geomancy is also known as Astronomical Geomancy and was one of the earliest forms of geomancy developed by ancient civilizations in Babylon, Egypt, and Greece. In this type of geomancy, a chart is created that shows the movement of celestial bodies in relation to each other at a given time and place. The chart is then used to determine what the future holds for an individual based on their birth date or time of birth.

Astrological geomancy uses constellations and other astronomical phenomena instead of elements on a map to generate predictions about future events. The most common version involves interpreting how specific constellations will look at sunrise in your location on a particular day to determine what will happen in your life over the next week, month, or year.

This type of geomancy was practiced in Europe until about 1550, when Pope Paul III prohibited it due to its association with magic and witchcraft. Today, there is a resurgence of interest in astrological Geomancy, and many modern practitioners believe that it can be used to gain insight into our lives, relationships, and career choices.

Many resources are available online and in libraries, if you are interested in exploring astrological geomancy. Start by finding a birth chart calculator so you can create your chart. Once you have your chart, take time to research the different placements and what they mean. The more you know about astrological geomancy, the more accurate your readings will be.

Numerological Geomancy

Numerology is the study of numbers and their influence on our lives. Each number has its energy and vibration that can impact our thoughts, feelings, and actions. Numerological Geomancy is the practice of using numbers to understand our lives and make predictions.

There are many different ways to calculate your numbers, but the most common method is to use your birth date. Once you have your numbers, you can start to interpret their meaning. Each number has a range of qualities associated with it, so you can use this information to gain insight into your personality, strengths, and challenges.

Numerological geomancy can be used for various purposes, such as understanding your relationships, making career choices, or predicting the future. You can find more information about this type of geomancy by doing an online search or visiting your local bookstores and libraries. Start by calculating your numbers, and then take some time to research their meanings.

Spiritual Geomancy

Few people know about spiritual geomancy, but it is a fascinating subject. It is the practice of using the earth's energy to heal and balance the mind, body, and spirit. Spiritual geomancy takes this one step further by using the earth's energy to connect with the spiritual realm. This can be done in many ways, but some of the most popular methods include meditating in nature, using crystals and stones, and working with plant spirits.

This type of geomancy is used to communicate with spirits and angels. The practitioner draws a mandala on the ground, representing the universe and its spiritual energy. The person then draws lines between each planet in the solar system and meditates on their questions before drawing them on paper or parchment. This type of geomancy can be used for a variety of purposes, such as guidance, protection, and healing.

Spiritual geomancy is based on astrology but focuses more on spiritual influences than physical ones. Spiritual geomancy uses astrological charts to determine how certain planets influence your life. It also looks at things like your birth date and time, and your name.

Like the other types, you'll find plenty of resources online or in libraries/book stores should you wish to learn more about spiritual geomancy. Start by finding a mandala or other symbol that resonates with you, and then take some time to research the different meanings. You may also want to find a quiet place in nature where you can meditate and connect with the earth's energy.

There are many different types of geomancy, each with its unique history and practice. The three most popular types of geomancy are astrological, numerological, and spiritual. Astrological geomancy is the practice of using the positions of celestial bodies to understand our lives. Numerological geomancy is the practice of using numbers to understand our lives. Spiritual geomancy is the practice of using the earth's energy to connect with the spiritual realm.

Geomantic Figures

Geomantic figures are shapes that are used in divination. A total of 16 figures were created by combining pairs of dots in various ways. Each figure has its meaning which can be interpreted according to the question at hand. For example, the figure known as "Populus" is typically associated with emotional turmoil, while "Acquisitio" represents gain and abundance.

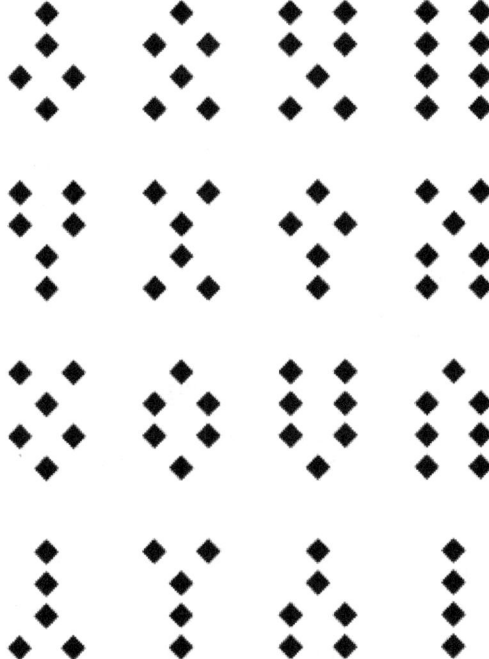

The 16 geomantic figures.
https://commons.wikimedia.org/wiki/File:Geomantic_figures.svg

Geomantic figures are made up of four parts:

1. **The Natal Square:** The natal square is the most important part of any reading. It shows how all the lines interact with each other and what they mean together.

2. **The Line:** Each line represents one path that your life can take. It may be positive or negative, but it will always affect your success, happiness, and overall well-being.

3. **The House:** Each house represents a different area of life. Some houses affect your career; others affect your love life,

and so on. Each house has its meaning and its own set of rules that must be followed when interpreting it correctly.

4. **The Element:** This element indicates how strongly each house affects you. If it is in detriment, this particular house will have little impact on your life, but if it is prominent, this house will have a huge impact on you.

Creating Geomantic Figures

There are many ways to create geomantic figures, but the most common method is dividing a square or circle into four equal parts. This can be done with a pencil and paper or by using a compass. Once the square or circle has been divided, the resulting quadrants can be subdivided similarly. This process is continued until there are 16 small squares or circles. These 16 figures are then interpreted according to their position within the overall design.

You will need a piece of paper and a pen to create a geomantic figure. Begin by drawing four lines of dots, making sure that each line contains an equal number of dots. Then, connect the dots in pairs to create the eight basic figures. Once you have the basic figures, you can combine them to create the other eight figures. Finally, you will need to interpret the meaning of each figure according to its position within the design.

Geomancy can be an enjoyable and rewarding activity for people of all ages. It can also be used as a tool for self-reflection and personal growth. If you are interested in exploring geomancy further, there are many resources available online and in libraries. Start by finding a mandala or other symbol that resonates with you, and then take some time to research the different meanings.

Interpreting Geomantic Figures

Geomantic figures can be used for divination to find hidden treasures or simply to admire the beauty of the earth's patterns. One must first understand the basics of line and form to interpret a geomantic figure. The most basic element of a geomantic figure is the line. Lines can be either straight or curved, and they can intersect or run parallel to one another.

The second basic element is formation; these can be either organic or geometric. Organic forms occur naturally, such as mountains, trees, and rivers; geometric forms are man-made, such as buildings, roads, and bridges. By studying the lines and forms of a geomantic figure, one can begin to see the hidden meaning within.

To interpret a geomantic figure, simply look up the meaning of the individual components and then piece together an answer to your question. With a little practice, you will be able to read geomantic figures with ease.

Geomancy in Practice

Geomancy is one of many forms of divination that uses a method called "reading the signs." It means interpreting patterns in the natural world around us. Geomancy can be done in any location, at any time, but it is best done outdoors. For this reason, it is often done at sunrise or sunset when light and shadows are most clear.

Although it may seem complicated at first, geomancy is quite simple. With a little practice, anyone can learn to read the signs of the earth.

There are two basic steps to geomancy, creating the figures and interpreting them. To create the figures, you will need a piece of paper and something to draw with. Begin by drawing 16 small squares in a 4×4 grid. Once the squares are drawn, randomly fill each square with one or two dots. This will create a figure known as a "mother."

Next, draw a line down the center of each column and row, splitting the mother into 16 smaller squares, or "daughters." Finally, count the dots in each daughter square and draw a line to connect any two squares that have the same number of dots. This will create your geomantic figure.

To interpret the figure, begin by looking at the overall shape. Is it curved or straight? Is it symmetrical or asymmetrical? Each type of shape corresponds to a different element, earth, air, fire, or water, and can provide clues about your question.

Next, look at the individual lines and forms within the figure. What do they remind you of? Do they create any patterns? Each line and form has a different meaning, so take some time to look up

the symbolism associated with each one.

Finally, consider the position of the figure within the design. Is it in the center or off to the side? Is it above or below the other figures? The position of a particular figure can provide clues about the timing of an event or the importance of a question.

Geomancy is an ancient practice that involves using patterns in the earth to gain insights into the future. Geomancers believe that the earth is alive and full of energy and that by reading its patterns, we can tap into its unlimited knowledge. By interpreting the stick's movement, the geomancer can gain insights into the future. Another popular method is to read the patterns formed by stones or leaves.

By studying the shapes and colors of these patterns, the geomancer can glean information about what is to come. Regardless of which method you use, geomancy can be a powerful tool to gain insight into the future.

Geomancy is a fascinating way to study the earth and its hidden meanings. Practiced by cultures worldwide, it is a great way to connect with the natural world. By understanding the basics of line and form, you can begin to interpret the hidden messages in the earth's patterns. With a little practice, anyone can learn to read the signs of the earth!

Chapter 2: Why Planets Matter

Are you curious about how the planets influence your day-to-day life? Do you want to know more about the connection between astrology and geomancy?

Astrology is the study of the movements and relative positions of celestial bodies interpreted as having an influence on human affairs and the natural world. Geomancy, on the other hand, is a form of divination that interprets markings on the earth, either in the sand or soil, to answer questions about the future. This chapter will explore the connection between these two ancient practices.

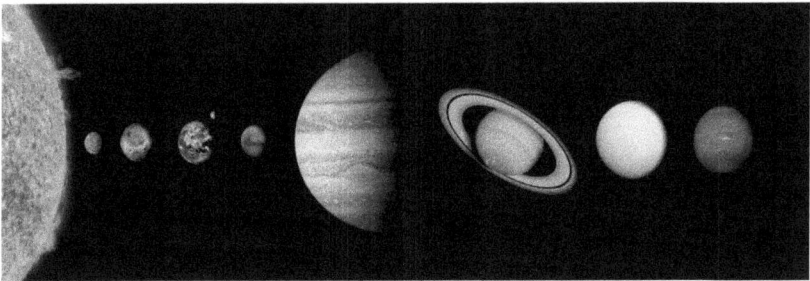

Astrology and geomancy go hand in hand.
https://pixabay.com/es/photos/sistema-solar-sol-mercurio-venus-439046/

We will explore the role of planets in geomancy and show you how to use astrology to interpret your geomantic readings. We will start with a brief overview of the importance of planets in geomancy, followed by an exploration of each planet and how its energy manifests.

Importance of Planets in Geomancy

Planets play an important role in geomancy, the study of the earth's energy field. By observing the positions of the planets, geomancers can identify patterns and relationships that can be used to interpret the earth's energy and make predictions about future events. The planets also influence the flow of energy within the earth, and by understanding these influences, geomancers can adjust their practices to maximize the positive effects of this energy.

In addition, the planets can be used as tools for divination that provide insight into the hidden forces at work in our lives. By understanding the symbolism and meaning of each planet, we can begin to understand the messages that the earth is trying to communicate to us.

How Planets Influence Geomantic Readings

Geomantic readings are used to interpret the energy of a specific location. This practice dates back centuries and is based on the belief that the land has a unique energy signature. By understanding this signature, we can gain insights into a particular place's past, present, and future. Many different factors can influence a geomantic reading, but one of the most important is the position of the planets.

Each planet has its energy, and when they are in alignment with certain points on the earth, they can amplify or diminish the power of that location. For example, if Mars is in alignment with a powerful geomantic point, it can intensify the energy of that point. Conversely, if Saturn is in alignment with a point of weakness, it can help dissipate its power. By taking the position of the planets into account, we can get a more accurate reading of the earth's energy signature.

Why Understanding Astrological Concepts Is Important for Geomancy

Astrology is the study of the movements and relative positions of celestial bodies interpreted as having an influence on human affairs and the natural world. The word "astrology" comes from the Greek words for "star" and "logos," which means "the word of God." Astrology has been used for centuries to help people understand the world around them, and it is still used today for a variety of purposes.

One of the key concepts of geomancy is the importance of understanding astrological principles. This is because the planets and stars have a tremendous impact on the Earth's energy field. By understanding how the planets and stars influence the Earth's energy, geomancers can make more informed decisions about where to place ley lines, align sacred sites, and maximize the benefits of planetary energies.

In addition, a thorough understanding of astrology can help geomancers predict potential problems and take steps to avoid them. As such, astrology is an essential tool for anyone interested in pursuing geomancy. The connection between these two ancient practices is undeniable. By understanding both, we can develop a deeper understanding of the earth's energy and position in it.

In the following sections, we will take a look at individual planets and how their energies influence geomancy.

The Sun: The Heart of Geomancy

Effects: Life-giving, Creative, Vital, Willpower

The sun is the most important planet in geomancy. It is the source of all life, and its energy is essential when it comes to sustaining the Earth's natural balance. The sun represents ego and willpower. When the sun is strong in a reading, it indicates that the individual has the potential to achieve great things. However, if the sun is weak, it indicates that the individual may need to put in more effort to realize their goals.

The sun's energy is also associated with creativity and self-expression. When the sun is strong, it indicates that the individual

has the potential to create something beautiful or to bring their unique talents to the world. However, if the sun is weak, it indicates that the individual may need to put in more effort to bring their creative vision to fruition.

The sun is also associated with vitality and health. When the sun is strong, it indicates that the individual has the potential to enjoy good health and vitality. However, if the sun is weak, it indicates that the individual may need to take better care of their health and put in more effort to maintain their vitality.

Symbolism

The sun is represented by a circle with a point in the center. This symbolizes the sun's life-giving energy and its creative potential. The sun is also associated with the color gold, which represents the sun's power and vitality. The sun is also associated with the element fire. This represents the sun's energy and its ability to transform and create.

Zodiac Signs Ruled by the Sun: Aries, Leo

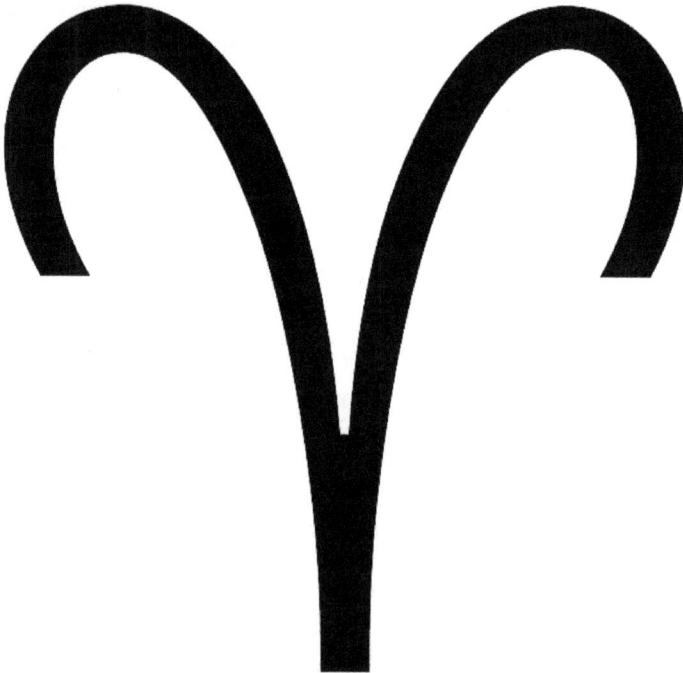

Aries is ruled by the sun.
https://pixabay.com/images/id-36388/

The Sun is considered to be the ruling planet of Leo. Leo is represented by the lion. People born under this sign are often said to be bold, ambitious, and confident. People ruled by the sun are also said to be natural leaders and are often very good at inspiring others. If you know someone who was born under the sign of Leo, you might find that they have a strong personality and are always up for a challenge.

The sun is also considered to be the ruling planet of Aries. It is represented by the ram. People born under this sign are often said to be impulsive, courageous, and competitive. People ruled by the sun are also said to be natural leaders and are often very good at taking charge. If you know someone born under Aries, you might find that they have a strong personality and are always up for a challenge.

Summary of the Sun

The sun is the most important planet in geomancy. It is the source of all life, and its energy is essential for sustaining the Earth's natural balance. The sun is a planet that should be approached with caution. Its energy is very powerful, and if it is not used correctly, it can hurt the individual's life.

In general, the sun is a positive influence on reading. Its energy is associated with growth, creativity, and self-expression. However, the sun can also be a difficult planet to handle. Its energy is very powerful, and if it is not used correctly, it can lead to egotism, narcissism, and a sense of entitlement.

Moon – Our Nearest Neighbor

Effects: Emotions, Gut Instincts, Nurturing, Feminine Energy

The moon is the second most important planet in geomancy. It is associated with emotions, gut instincts, and nurturing. The moon represents the subconscious mind, and its energy is often more powerful than the conscious mind. The moon is also associated with feminine energy, and its energy is more watery and fluid than the masculine one of the sun.

The moon's energy is more passive and receptive than that of the sun. The moon is associated with intuition and feelings, and its energy is more compassionate and nurturing. The moon's energy is

also more nightmarish than that of the sun. The moon is associated with addiction, obsession, and mental illness.

Symbolism

The moon is represented by a crescent, symbolizing the moon's connection to emotions and intuition. It is also associated with the color silver. This represents the moon's connection to emotions and intuition. It is also associated with the element water. It represents the moon's fluid and changeable energy.

Zodiac Signs Ruled by the Moon: Cancer, Pisces

The moon is the ruling planet of cancer.
https://pixabay.com/images/id-2551431/

The moon is considered to be the ruling planet of Cancer, represented by the crab. People born under this sign are often emotional, intuitive, and nurturing. People ruled by the moon are also very in tune with their feelings and are often quite good at understanding other people's emotions.

The moon is also considered to be the ruling planet of Pisces. The fish represent Pisces. People born under this sign are often compassionate, adaptable, and imaginative. This sign is said to be the most intuitive of all the zodiac signs, and people ruled by the moon are often very in tune with their emotions.

Summary of the Moon

The moon is the second most important planet in geomancy. It is associated with emotions, gut instincts, and nurturing. The moon represents the subconscious mind, and its energy is often more powerful than the conscious mind. The moon is also associated with feminine energy, and its energy is more watery and fluid than the masculine one of the sun.

In general, the moon is a positive influence in readings. Its energy is associated with intuition, compassion, and creativity. However, the moon can also be a difficult planet to handle. Its energy is very powerful, and if it is not used correctly, it can lead to addiction, obsession, and mental illness.

Mercury – The Messenger

Effects: Communication, Intelligence, Travel

Mercury is the third most important planet in geomancy. It is associated with communication, intelligence, and travel. Mercury represents the conscious mind, and its energy is often more active and analytical than the subconscious mind. Mercury is also associated with the element of air. This represents Mercury's connection to communication and ideas.

Mercury's energy is more mental than emotional. This planet is associated with logic and reason, and its energy is more cerebral than the emotional one of the moon. Mercury is also associated with commerce and transportation.

Symbolism

Mercury is represented by a winged messenger. This symbolizes Mercury's connection to communication and travel. It is also associated with the color green. This represents its connection to growth, fertility, and nature.

Zodiac Signs Ruled by Mercury: Gemini, Virgo

Gemini is ruled by Mercury.
https://pixabay.com/images/id-2550197/

Mercury is considered the ruling planet of Gemini and is represented by the twins. People born under this sign are often good at communication, very social, and quite adaptable. Gemini is also said to be the most intelligent of all the zodiac signs, and people ruled by Mercury are often very quick-witted and sharp.

Mercury is also considered to be the ruling planet of Virgo and is represented by the virgin. People born under this sign are often hard-working, practical, and detail-oriented. Virgo is also said to be the most grounded of all the zodiac signs, and people ruled by Mercury are often very level-headed and down-to-earth.

Summary of Mercury

Mercury is the third most important planet in geomancy. It is associated with communication, intelligence, and travel. Mercury represents the conscious mind, and its energy is often more active and analytical than the subconscious mind. Mercury is also associated with the element of air. This represents Mercury's connection to communication and ideas.

Venus – The Lover

Effects: Love, Beauty, Money

Venus is the fourth most important planet in geomancy. It is associated with love, beauty, and money. Venus represents the heart, and its energy is often more romantic and emotional than the mind. Venus is also associated with the element of earth. This represents Venus's connection to the physical world.

Symbolism

Venus is represented by the goddess of love. This symbolizes Venus's connection to love and beauty. Venus is also associated with the color pink. This represents Venus's connection to romance and femininity. With its ruling planet in the sign of Gemini, Venus brings an added element of adaptability to love and relationships.

Zodiac Signs Ruled by Venus: Taurus, Libra

Venus is the ruling planet of Taurus.
https://pixabay.com/images/id-2552502/

Venus is considered to be the ruling planet of Taurus, represented by the bull. People born under this sign are often reliable, patient, and hard-working. Taurus is also said to be the most down-to-earth of all the zodiac signs, and people ruled by Venus are often very sensual and materialistic.

Venus is also considered to be the ruling planet of Libra. Libra is represented by scales. People born under this sign are often diplomatic, fair-minded, and social. Libra is also said to be the most idealistic of all the zodiac signs, and people ruled by Venus are often very romantic and good at relationships.

Summary of Venus

Venus is associated with love, beauty, and money. Venus represents the heart, and its energy is often more romantic and emotional than the mind. Venus is also associated with the element of earth. This represents Venus' connection to the physical world. With its ruling planet in the sign of Gemini, Venus brings an added element of adaptability to love and relationships.

Mars – The Warrior

Effects: Action, Energy, Passion

The planet Mars is named after the Roman god of war. Mars is associated with action, energy, and passion. Mars represents the will, and its energy is often forceful and aggressive. Mars is also associated with the element of fire. This represents Mars' connection to energy and passion. It is also associated with the color red. This represents Mars' connection to action and assertiveness.

Symbolism

Mars is represented by the god of war. This symbolizes Mars' connection to action and aggression. Mars is also associated with iron. This represents its connection to strength and power. The symbol for Mars is a spear, which represents Mars' connection to assertiveness and courage.

Zodiac Signs Ruled by Mars: Aries, Scorpio

Mars is considered the ruling planet of Scorpio.
https://pixabay.com/images/id-2782164/

Mars is considered to be the ruling planet of Aries. It is represented by the ram. People born under this sign are often impulsive, enthusiastic, and competitive. Aries is also said to be the most independent of all the zodiac signs, and people ruled by Mars are often very self-assertive and headstrong.

Mars is also considered to be the ruling planet of Scorpio. Scorpio is represented by the scorpion. People born under this sign are often intense, passionate, and resourceful. Scorpio is also said to be the most mysterious of all the zodiac signs, and people ruled by Mars are often very private and secretive.

Summary of Mars

Mars is associated with action, energy, and passion. It represents the will, and its energy is often forceful and aggressive. Mars is also associated with the element fire. This represents Mars' connection to energy and passion. With its ruling planet in the sign of Aries, Mars brings an added element of independence to action and assertiveness.

Jupiter – The Planet of Luck

Effects: Expansion, Optimism, Opportunity

The planet Jupiter is named after the Roman god of luck. Jupiter is associated with expansion, optimism, and opportunity. It represents the principle of growth, and its energy is often optimistic and generous. Jupiter is also associated with the element of fire. This represents Jupiter's connection to growth and expansion. The color purple is also associated with Jupiter. This represents its connection to wisdom and knowledge.

Symbolism

The symbol for Jupiter is a thunderbolt, which represents Jupiter's connection to power and authority. Jupiter is also associated with tin. This represents its connection to luck and fortune. Thursday is also associated with Jupiter. This represents its connection to abundance and prosperity.

Zodiac Signs Ruled by Jupiter: Sagittarius, Pisces

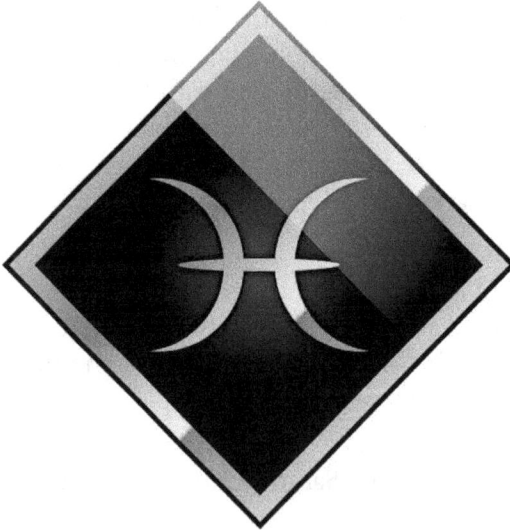

Pisces is ruled by Jupiter.
https://pixabay.com/images/id-2782348/

Jupiter is considered to be the ruling planet of Sagittarius. Sagittarius is represented by the archer. People born under this sign are often optimistic, independent, and adventurous. Sagittarius is also the most idealistic of all the zodiac signs. People ruled by

Jupiter are often very positive and strongly believe in justice.

Jupiter is also considered to be the ruling planet of Pisces. Pisces is represented by the fish. People born under this sign are often compassionate, imaginative, and sensitive. Pisces is also the most spiritual of all the zodiac signs, and people ruled by Jupiter are often very intuitive and in touch with their higher selves.

Summary of Jupiter

Jupiter is associated with expansion, optimism, and opportunity. Jupiter represents the principle of growth, and its energy is often optimistic and generous. Jupiter is also associated with the element of fire. This represents Jupiter's connection to growth and expansion. With its ruling planet in the sign of Sagittarius, Jupiter brings an added element of adventure and idealism to action.

Saturn – The Planet of Responsibility

Effects: Structure, Discipline, Restriction

The planet Saturn is named after the Roman god of time. Saturn is associated with structure, discipline, and restriction. Saturn represents the principle of limitation, and its energy is often serious and sober. Saturn is also associated with the element of earth. This represents Saturn's connection to stability and endurance. The color black is also associated with Saturn. This represents its connection to darkness and mystery.

Symbolism

The symbol for Saturn is a cross, which represents its connection to responsibility and duty. It is also associated with lead. This represents Saturn's connection to heaviness and density. Saturday is also associated with Saturn. This represents its connection to structure and discipline.

Zodiac Signs Ruled by Saturn: Capricorn, Aquarius

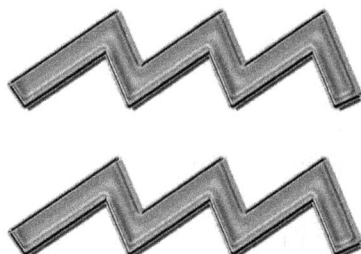

Aquarius is ruled by Saturn.
https://pixabay.com/images/id-3915988/

Saturn is considered to be the ruling planet of Capricorn. Capricorn is represented by the goat. People under this sign are often ambitious, hard-working, and practical. Capricorn is also the most disciplined of all the zodiac signs, and people ruled by Saturn are often very responsible and reliable.

Saturn is also considered to be the ruling planet of Aquarius. It is represented by the water bearer. People born under this sign are often humanitarian, progressive, and eccentric. Aquarius is also the most unconventional of all the zodiac signs, and people ruled by Saturn are often very independent and original.

Summary of Saturn

Saturn is associated with structure, discipline, and responsibility. It represents the principle of limitation, and its energy is often serious and sober. Saturn is also associated with the element earth. This represents its connection to stability and endurance. With its ruling planet in the sign of Capricorn, Saturn brings an added element of ambition and practicality to action.

Lunar Nodes – The Dragon's Head and Tail

The Lunar Nodes are two points in space where the Moon's orbit intersects with the Earth's orbit around the Sun. The point where the orbits intersect is called the node. The Lunar Nodes are also sometimes referred to as the Dragon's Head and Tail.

The North Node is considered the Dragon's Head, and the South Node is considered the Dragon's Tail. The North Node is associated with future potential, and the South Node is associated with *experience.*

The Lunar Nodes are also said to be the points of karmic destiny. The North Node is said to represent our soul's mission in this lifetime, and the South Node is said to represent our soul's karma from past lifetimes.

Symbolism

The symbol for the Lunar Nodes is two circles connected by a line. The line represents the path of destiny, and the circles represent the Dragon's Head and Tail. The North Node is associated with the element fire, and the South Node is associated with the element of water. This represents the opposing energies of the Lunar Nodes.

Zodiac Signs Ruled by the Lunar Nodes: Cancer, Capricorn

Capricon is ruled by the lunar nodes.
https://pixabay.com/images/id-2782396/

The Lunar Nodes are said to be the rulers of Cancer and Capricorn. Cancer is represented by the crab. People born under this sign are often emotional, sensitive, and nurturing. Cancer is also a sign of the home, and people ruled by the Lunar Nodes are often very family-oriented.

The goat represents Capricorn, and people born under this sign are often ambitious, hard-working, and practical. Capricorn is also a sign of responsibility, and people ruled by the Lunar Nodes are often very reliable.

Summary of the Lunar Nodes

The Lunar Nodes are not planets, but they are considered to be very important points in space. They are said to have a powerful influence on our lives and are often studied in astrology and karma. The Lunar Nodes are said to be the points of karmic destiny and represent our soul's mission in this lifetime.

The planets and other celestial bodies profoundly influence our lives, both in terms of our personalities and the larger events that shape our world. By understanding the planets' symbolism and meaning, we can better understand ourselves and the universe around us.

Chapter 3: The Elements and the Zodiac Signs

Do you ever wonder why people act the way they do? Or why you are drawn to certain types of people? Perhaps it has something to do with the stars. In this chapter, we will explore the spiritual side of zodiac signs and discover the meaning behind each element.

There are four elements in astrology, fire, earth, air, and water. Each element is associated with a set of qualities. All zodiac signs belong to one of these elements. This chapter is divided into four sections, one for each element. We will begin with a general overview of the element, followed by a keywords list, symbol, and description of the associated zodiac signs.

All zodiac signs fall under an element.
https://pixabay.com/es/photos/reloj-hist%c3%b3rico-praga-ciudad-1096054/

You will learn about the keywords, symbols, and traits associated with fire (Aries, Leo, and Sagittarius), earth (Taurus, Virgo, and Capricorn), air (Gemini, Libra, and Aquarius), and water (Cancer, Pisces, and Scorpio) zodiac signs. By the end of this chapter, you will have a greater understanding of yourself and others.

Spiritual Meaning of Zodiac Signs

Each zodiac sign has its own unique set of characteristics and traits. But did you know that each one has a spiritual meaning as well? For example, Aries is associated with new beginnings, while Pisces is associated with compassion and forgiveness.

By understanding your zodiac sign's spiritual meaning, you can better understand yourself and your place in the world. So, what is the spiritual meaning of your zodiac sign? Read on to find out.

Fire: Aries, Leo, and Sagittarius

Keywords: Action, Assertiveness, Passion, Creativity

Symbol of Fire Element: The Triangle

The element of fire is associated with qualities such as passion, courage, and determination. Fire signs are known for their high energy and enthusiasm. If you are drawn to people with these qualities, it is likely because you are a fire sign yourself.

Fire signs are also associated with the astrological houses of the self (First House), creativity (Fifth House), and spirituality (Ninth House). The planet Mars rules people with fire signs. The red planet is associated with energy, action, and assertiveness.

Zodiac Signs Associated with Fire

Three zodiac signs are associated with fire, Aries, Leo, and Sagittarius. People of these signs are said to be passionate, dynamic, and full of energy. They tend to be natural leaders and are often drawn to careers that involve taking risks. People with these signs are also known for their sense of adventure and may enjoy traveling or engaging in outdoor activities.

While people with these zodiac signs can be warm and loving, they can also be quick-tempered and impulsive. However, their fierce determination and optimistic attitude usually help them overcome any obstacle that comes their way.

Aries

Traits: Adventurous, Natural Leaders, Determined

Aries is the first sign of the zodiac, and it is associated with new beginnings. People who have this sign are said to be natural leaders. They are often drawn to careers that involve taking risks and may enjoy traveling or engaging in outdoor activities.

Aries people are also known for their sense of adventure and may be impulsive and quick-tempered. However, their fierce determination and optimistic attitude usually help them overcome any obstacle that comes their way.

Symbolism: The Ram

The symbol for Aries is a ram, which represents assertiveness, courage, and determination. In Greek mythology, the ram was associated with Olympus, the home of the gods. This connection gives Aries an added sense of nobility and grandeur. Whether you are an Aries yourself or you know someone who is, you can not help but be drawn to their energy and strength of character.

Leo

Traits: Generous, Creative, Warm-hearted, Loyal

Leo is the fifth sign of the zodiac and is associated with the astrological house of creativity (Fifth House). People who have this sign are creative and warm-hearted. They tend to be natural leaders and are often drawn to careers that involve taking risks.

People with these signs are also known for their sense of adventure and may enjoy traveling or engaging in outdoor activities. While people with these zodiac signs can be impulsive and quick-tempered, their fierce determination and optimistic attitude usually help them overcome any obstacle that comes their way.

Symbolism: The Lion

The lion is the symbol of Leo, and it represents courage, strength, and royalty. The lion is a noble creature that is often associated with the sun. In Greek mythology, the lion was also associated with Olympus, the home of the gods. The link between Leo and the sun gives Leo an added sense of warmth and generosity.

Sagittarius

Traits: Independent, Optimistic, Truth-seekers

Sagittarius is the ninth sign of the zodiac and is associated with the astrological house of spirituality (Ninth House). People who have this sign are independent and optimistic. They tend to be natural truth-seekers and are often drawn to careers that involve taking risks.

People with this sign are known for their sense of humor and their love of travel. Sagittarius is a fire sign, and the planet Jupiter rules people with this sign. Jupiter is associated with good fortune, expansion, and abundance.

Symbolism: The Archer

The archer is the symbol of Sagittarius, and it represents truth-seeking and optimism. The archer is also associated with the planet Jupiter, which gives Sagittarius its upbeat attitude. With the archer as their symbol, people with this sign always aim for the stars.

Earth: (Taurus, Virgo, and Capricorn)

Keywords: Grounded, Practical, Reliable

Symbol of the Earth: The Pentacle

Earth signs are grounded, practical, and reliable. They are often drawn to careers that involve helping others and may enjoy working with their hands. People with these signs are patient and methodical but can also be inflexible and stubborn.

Earth signs are ruled by the planet Saturn, which is associated with discipline, responsibility, and hard work. The symbol for earth is a pentacle, which represents the material world. A pentacle is a five-pointed star that is enclosed in a circle. The star's five points represent the five elements: earth, air, fire, water, and spirit.

In Greek mythology, the earth was associated with Demeter, the goddess of the harvest. Demeter was a kind and generous goddess, but she could also be stern and inflexible. The link between the earth and Demeter gives those with earth signs their practical and reliable nature.

Taurus

Traits: Reliable, Patient, Practical, Sensual

Taurus is the second sign of the zodiac and is associated with the

astrological house of material possessions (Second House). People who have this sign are reliable and patient. They tend to be practical and down-to-earth and are often drawn to careers that involve security and stability.

People with this sign are also known for their love of sensual pleasures. Taurus is an earth sign, and people with this sign are ruled by the planet Venus. Venus is associated with love, beauty, and pleasure. It is also linked to the goddess Aphrodite, who was known for her beauty and sensuality.

Symbolism: The Bull

The bull is the symbol of Taurus, and it represents dependability, patience, and practicality. The bull is also associated with the planet Venus, which gives Taurus its love of beauty and pleasure. The bull is a gentle creature but can also be stubborn and inflexible. This combination of qualities makes Taurus a reliable and down-to-earth sign.

Virgo

Traits: Analytical, Loyal, Hardworking, Practical

Virgo is the sixth sign of the zodiac and is associated with the astrological house of work and health (Sixth House). People who have this sign are analytical and hard-working. They tend to be loyal and practical and are often drawn to careers that involve helping others.

People with this sign are also known for their attention to detail. Virgo is an earth sign, and people with this sign are ruled by the planet Mercury. Mercury is associated with communication, commerce, and travel. It is also linked to the god Hermes, who was known for his cunning and wit.

Symbolism: The Virgin

The virgin is the symbol of Virgo, and it represents purity, innocence, and virginity. The virgin is also associated with the planet Mercury, which gives Virgo its attention to detail and analytical mind. The virgin is a pure and innocent creature, but can also be complex and mysterious. This combination of qualities makes Virgo an analytical and hard-working sign.

Capricorn

Traits: Ambitious, Driven, Persistent, Resourceful

Capricorn is the tenth sign of the zodiac and is associated with the astrological house of career and ambition (Tenth House). People who have this sign are ambitious and driven. They tend to be persistent and resourceful and are often drawn to careers involving power and status.

People with this sign are also known for their discipline and self-control. Capricorn is an earth sign, and people with this sign are ruled by the planet Saturn. Saturn is associated with responsibility, hard work, and discipline. It is also linked to the god Cronus, who was known for his strength and power.

Symbolism: The Goat

The goat is the symbol of Capricorn, and it represents ambition, persistence, and resourcefulness. The goat is also associated with the planet Saturn, which gives Capricorn its discipline and self-control. The goat is a hard-working and determined creature, but it can also be stubborn and inflexible. This combination of qualities makes Capricorn an ambitious and driven sign.

Air: Gemini, Libra, Aquarius

Keywords: Communication, Intellectualism, Social Interactions.

Symbol for the Air Element: The Winged Messenger

Air signs are associated with the astrological houses of communication (Third House) and social interactions (Eleventh House). People with air signs are often known for their communication skills and intellectualism. They tend to be social and outgoing and are often drawn to careers involving networking and social interactions.

The symbol for air is the winged messenger, who represents communication and intellectualism. The messenger is also associated with the planet Mercury, which gives air signs the communication skills and social nature. The messenger is a quick and agile creature, but it can also be scattered and unfocused in nature. It is this combination of qualities that makes air signs social and intellectual.

Gemini

Traits: Adaptable, Communicative, Inquisitive, Social

Gemini is the third sign of the zodiac and is associated with the astrological house of communication (Third House). People with this sign are known for their communication skills and inquisitive nature. They tend to be adaptable and social and are often drawn to careers involving networking and social interactions.

People with this sign are also known for their dual nature. Gemini is an air sign, and people with this sign are ruled by the planet Mercury. Mercury is associated with communication, commerce, and travel. It is also linked to the god Hermes, who was known for his cunning and wit.

Symbolism: The Twins

The twins are the symbol of Gemini and represent communication and duality. The twins are also associated with the planet Mercury, which gives Gemini its communication skills and inquisitive nature. The twins are quick and agile creatures but can also be scattered and unfocused. This combination of qualities makes Gemini an adaptable and communicative sign.

Libra

Traits: Balanced, Diplomatic, Fair-minded, Social

Libra is the seventh sign of the zodiac and is associated with the astrological house of relationships (Seventh House). People with this sign are often known for their diplomacy and social nature. They tend to be fair-minded and balanced and are often drawn to careers involving networking and social interactions.

People with this sign are also known for their indecision. Libra is an air sign, and people with this sign are ruled by the planet Venus. Venus is associated with love, beauty, and relationships. It is also linked to the goddess Aphrodite, who was known for her beauty and charm.

Symbolism: The Scales

The scales are Libra's symbol, representing balance and relationships. The scales are also associated with the planet Venus, which gives Libra its diplomatic and social nature. The scales are a stable and reliable creature, but they can also be indecisive and changeable. This combination of qualities makes Libra a balanced

and fair-minded sign.

Aquarius

Traits: Eccentric, Friendly, Humanitarian, Independent

Aquarius is the eleventh sign of the zodiac, and it is associated with the astrological house of social interactions (Eleventh House). People with this sign are often known for their eccentricity and humanitarianism. They tend to be independent and friendly and are often drawn to careers involving networking and social interactions.

People with this sign are also known for their unpredictable nature. Aquarius is an air sign, and people with this sign are ruled by the planet Uranus. Uranus is associated with change, freedom, and innovation. It is also linked to the god Zeus, who was known for his power and strength.

Symbolism: The Water Bearer

The water bearer is the symbol of Aquarius, and it represents eccentricity and humanitarianism. The water bearer is also associated with the planet Uranus, which gives Aquarius its unpredictable nature. The water bearer is a creative and unconventional creature, but they can also be aloof and detached. This combination of qualities makes Aquarius an eccentric and independent sign.

Water: Cancer, Pisces, Scorpio

Keywords for Water Element: Emotional, Intuitive, Compassionate, Nurturing, Imaginative, Sensitive.

Symbol for the Water Element: The Cup

Water signs are associated with the astrological houses of emotions (Fourth House) and imagination (Twelfth House). People with water signs are often known for their emotions and imagination. They tend to be compassionate and nurturing and are often drawn to careers that involve caring for others.

People with water signs are also known for their sensitivity. Water signs are ruled by the planet Neptune and the Moon. The Moon is associated with emotions, while Neptune is associated with imagination. Water signs are obviously linked to the element of water, which is associated with emotions and intuition.

The cup is the symbol of water, and it represents emotions and imagination. The cup is also associated with the planet Neptune, which gives water signs their sensitivity. The cup is a receptacle for emotions, and it is also a source of nourishment. It is this combination of qualities that makes water signs compassionate and nurturing.

Cancer

Traits: Emotional, Intuitive, Compassionate, Nurturing

Cancer is the fourth sign of the zodiac and is associated with the astrological house of emotions (Fourth House). People with this sign are often known for their emotions and compassion. They tend to be nurturing and intuitive and are often drawn to careers that involve caring for others.

People with this sign are also known for their sensitivity. Cancer is a water sign, and people with this sign are ruled by the planet Moon. The Moon is associated with emotions. Cancer is also linked to the element of water, which is associated with intuition.

Symbolism: The Crab

The crab is the symbol of Cancer, and it represents emotions and compassion. The crab is also associated with the planet Moon, which gives Cancer its sensitivity. The crab is a hard-working and loyal creature but can also be moody and withdrawn. This combination of qualities makes Cancer an emotional and compassionate sign.

Pisces

Traits: Emotional, Intuitive, Compassionate, Nurturing, Imaginative

Pisces is the twelfth sign of the zodiac, and it is associated with the astrological house of imagination (Twelfth House). People with this sign are often known for their imagination and compassion. They tend to be nurturing and intuitive and are often drawn to careers that involve caring for others.

People with this sign are also known for their sensitivity. Pisces is a water sign, and the planet Neptune rules people with this sign. Neptune is associated with imagination. Pisces is also linked to the element of water, which is associated with intuition.

Symbolism: The Fish

The fish is the symbol of Pisces, and it represents imagination and compassion. The fish is also associated with the planet Neptune, which gives Pisces its sensitivity. The fish is a creative and imaginative creature but can also easily be distracted. This combination of qualities makes Pisces a compassionate and imaginative sign.

Scorpio

Traits: Emotional, Intuitive, Passionate, Nurturing, Sensitive

Scorpio is the eighth sign of the zodiac and is associated with the astrological house of emotions (Fourth House). People with this sign are often known for their emotions and passion. They tend to be nurturing and intuitive and are often drawn to careers that involve caring for others.

People with this sign are also known for their sensitivity. Scorpio is a water sign, and planet Pluto rules people with this sign. Pluto is associated with passion. Scorpio is also linked to the element of water, which is associated with intuition.

Symbolism: The Scorpion

The scorpion is Scorpio's symbol, representing passion and emotion. The scorpion is also associated with the planet Pluto, which gives Scorpio its sensitivity. The scorpion is a passionate and intense creature but can also be jealous and possessive in nature. This combination of qualities makes Scorpio a sign of passion and emotion.

The spiritual meaning of the zodiac signs and their elements can be used to help understand people's personalities. The four elements, fire, earth, air, and water represent different qualities associated with the twelve zodiac signs.

Fire signs are associated with qualities such as passion and energy, while earth signs are associated with qualities such as stability and practicality. Air signs are associated with qualities such as intelligence and communication, while water signs are associated with qualities such as emotion and intuition.

Each sign is ruled by a planet, with each planet giving the signs their unique qualities. For example, Mars gives Aries its fiery energy, while Venus gives Libra its diplomatic charm. Neptune gives

Pisces its imaginative nature, while Pluto gives Scorpio its intense passion.

By understanding the meaning of the zodiac signs and their elements, we can better understand people's personalities. People are complex, and no one sign can describe a person perfectly. However, by looking at the elements and planets associated with each sign, we can get a general idea of what qualities each one represents.

Chapter 4: The Geomantic Houses

Do you want to learn about the geomantic houses? Are you familiar with any of the 12 geomantic houses? These 12 houses originated in Babylonian astrology and were later adopted by the Greeks. They are a fundamental piece of knowledge one should have to interpret a geomantic chart. While the astrological houses deal with planetary energies, the geomantic houses deal with the energies of the Earth.

In this chapter, we will discuss the meaning and significance of the astrological houses. You will learn about the 12 houses and their rulers. We will also touch on the three "extra" geomantic houses: the two witnesses and the judge. By the end of this chapter, you will have a better understanding of the geomantic houses and how they can be used to interpret a geomantic chart.

Introduction to Geomantic Houses

If you are just getting started with geomancy, you may be wondering what all the fuss is about with these houses. After all, are they not just a way to divide the sky into manageable sections? While that is certainly one way to think about them, there is a lot more to geomantic houses than meets the eye. Understanding how to use houses is essential to interpreting a geomantic chart properly.

Each of the 12 houses corresponds to a different area of life, and each one is associated with a different planet and zodiac sign. This means that when you are looking at a geomantic chart, you can get a sense of which areas of life are being affected by which planets. For example, if you see a planet in the first house, it indicates that there are currently some major changes taking place in your life. If you see a planet in the seventh house, it indicates that relationships are playing an important role in your current situation.

Of course, this is just a very basic introduction to geomantic houses. There is a lot more to learn if you want to get the most out of this ancient system of divination. But even if you only have a basic understanding of houses, you can still use them to get valuable insights into your life.

The 12 Geomantic Houses

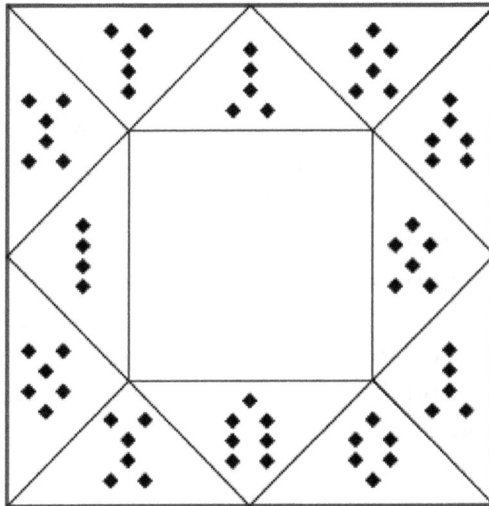

Geomantic house chart.
https://commons.wikimedia.org/wiki/File:Geomantic_housechart.svg

Now that we have briefly introduced the concept of geomantic houses, let's take a more in-depth look at each of the 12 houses. Remember, each house corresponds to a different area of life, so you will want to pay attention to the areas of your life that are most affected by the planets in each house.

The houses are each divided into three groups of four houses. The first group, known as the angular houses, comprises the 1st,

4th, 7th, and 10th houses. These are the most important houses in a geomantic chart, as they represent the areas of life that are most affected by the planets.

The second group, known as the succedent houses, comprises the 2nd, 5th, 8th, and 11th houses. These houses represent the areas of life that are the second most affected by the planets. The third group, known as the cadent houses, comprises the 3rd, 6th, 9th, and 12th houses. These houses represent the areas of life that are the least affected by the planets.

The angular houses govern the areas of life most important to you, while the cadent houses govern the areas of life least important to you. The succedent houses fall somewhere in between, governing the areas of life that are somewhat important to you. Now that you know how the houses are divided, let us look at each one in more detail.

The 1st House: House of Self

If you are looking to understand yourself better, the 1st house is a great place to start. Also known as the House of Self, this astrological house is all about your identity and how you present yourself to the world. It is also closely linked with your physical appearance, so if you want to make changes to your look, the 1st house can offer some insight into that area.

To further explore the 1st house, take a look at your birth chart. The sign occupying this house will give you clues about the areas of your life that are most important to you. For example, if Aries is in your 1st house, you may be especially driven and ambitious. Or, if Cancer is in this house, you may place a high value on family and home life.

The first house, also known as the ascendant, is associated with the planet Mars and the zodiac sign Aries. This house represents your individuality and how you relate to the world around you. By understanding the energy of the 1st house, you can better understand who you are and what makes you unique.

The 2nd House: House of Possessions

The 2nd house is all about possessions and material wealth. This includes not only your physical possessions but also your financial resources, skills and talents, and anything else you see as valuable. In a way, the 2nd house is a measure of your self-worth. Do you see yourself as wealthy or poor? Do you have a lot to offer the world, or do you feel like you have nothing to offer?

The 2nd house is also about how you handle your possessions. Are you a hoarder or a minimalist? Do you take care of your belongings, or do you let them fall into disrepair? The 2nd house reminds us that our possessions are not permanent but subject to change and misfortune. Therefore, it is important to use our possessions wisely and to remember that they are not what ultimately gives our lives value.

The 3rd House: House of Communications

The 3rd house is all about communication and the exchange of ideas. This includes spoken language, written language, body language, and any other form of communication. It also includes our relationship with knowledge and learning. Do we like to learn new things or prefer to stick to what we already know?

The 3rd house is also about our immediate environment and the people we interact with on a daily basis. This includes our siblings, our neighbors, and our co-workers. The 3rd house is a reminder that we are constantly interacting with the world around us and that our interactions significantly impact our lives.

The 4th House: House of Home and Family

The 4th house is commonly referred to as the house of home and family. This is because this house governs our domestic life, our roots, and our sense of belonging. The fourth house cusp (the line that divides the 4th house and the 3rd house) represents our childhood, and the plants in this house represent our parents and grandparents. The fourth house is also traditionally associated with the element of water, which symbolizes emotion, intuition, and creativity.

When we balance the energies of the 4th house, we create a supportive foundation for ourselves and our loved ones. We feel a sense of stability and security and express ourselves more freely. Our connection to our roots strengthens, and we nurture our relationships with others more effectively. The 4th house is a reminder that our family and home are our refuges from the outside world and that they should be treated with care.

The 5th House: House of Creativity

The fifth house is the House of Creativity, which pertains to all self-expression forms. This includes art, music, writing, and other activities that allow us to share our talents with the world. The fifth house symbolizes children and is associated with pregnancy and childbirth. In a more general sense, the fifth house represents all forms of pleasure and enjoyment. It is linked to joyful experiences such as vacations, parties, and any other form of entertainment.

When planets are located in the fifth house, they bring forth creative energies that can be used in constructive ways. However, if the planets are in challenging positions, they can create difficulties with self-expression or cause problems with fertility. Overall, the fifth house is a place of fun and creativity, and it reminds us to enjoy the good things in life.

The 6th House: House of Health and Work

The 6th house is associated with health and work. It is believed that Mercury governs this house and that Virgo is especially relevant. People with a strong 6th house influence are often hard workers who take pride in their achievements. They may be well-organized and detail-oriented, but they can also be overly perfectionist or critical.

Health is also important for people with a strong 6th house influence. They may be interested in nutrition and fitness and be careful about maintaining a healthy lifestyle. However, they can also be prone to worry and stress, which can take a toll on their physical well-being. Ultimately, the 6th house is a complex and intriguing energy field that sheds light on many aspects of our lives.

The 7th House: House of Balance

In astrology, the 7th house is associated with balance. This is the house of relationships, and it is through our relationships that we learn to find balance in our lives. The energy of the 7th house helps us see both sides of every situation and to find a middle ground between our own needs and those of others. It is also the house of compromise, teaching us that sometimes we have to give up something to gain something else.

In short, the 7th house helps us create harmony in our lives. When this house is strong in our birth chart, we can build satisfying and supportive relationships. We are also good at finding win-win solutions to conflicts.

If this house is weak in our chart, we may have difficulty seeing both sides of an issue, or we may find it hard to let go of our own needs to meet the needs of others. We may also struggle with making compromises. However, by working with the energy of the 7th house, we can learn to find balance in our lives.

The 8th House: House of Transformation

The 8th house is known as the House of Transformation. This is the house of death and rebirth, and it is associated with the planet Pluto. An 8th house is a place of power, and it is through this house that we learn to transform our lives. This house teaches us that change is an essential part of life and that we must learn to let go of the past to move forward.

The 8th house is also linked to sex, and through this house, we can learn to create new life. This house is about passion and intimacy, and it reminds us that sex is a sacred act of creation. Ultimately, the 8th house is a place of great power, and it teaches us that change is an essential part of life. If we can learn to embrace the energy of this house, we can transform our lives in profound and wonderful ways.

The 9th House: House of Higher Learning

The 9th house is associated with higher learning, and those who have planets in this house are often drawn to fields of study that require deep understanding and concentration. This may include academic subjects such as philosophy, religion, or the law. But it also encompasses more creative pursuits such as literature, poetry, and art.

Those with planets in the 9th house often have a deep need to explore the big questions in life, and they may find themselves spending hours lost in thought or absorbed in contemplation. To the outside world, they may appear aloof or even arrogant, but this is simply their way of processing the information they take in. They are constantly seeking knowledge, and their minds are always whirring with new ideas.

The 10th House: House of Career

The 10th House is commonly referred to as the House of Career. This is because it is associated with professional achievements, reputation, and public status. In a birth chart, the 10th House is located on the Midheaven, which is the highest point in the sky. This position symbolizes our highest aspirations and ambitions.

The planets and signs that occupy the 10th House reveal how we will go about achieving our goals and what kind of success we are likely to experience. For example, a planet in the 10th House may indicate that we will achieve our goals through our hard work and perseverance. Alternatively, a planet in this House may suggest that we will receive help from influential people or that we will have a natural talent for a particular profession.

Regardless of the planets involved, the 10th House always represents our drive to achieve success in the public eye. Through this House, we learn to take our place in the world and make our mark on society.

The 11th House: House of Friendships

In astrology, the 11th House is known as the House of Friendships. It represents our social circle and the relationships we have with others. This House is all about connection and community. We often think of our friends as family, and this house reflects just that. It reminds us that we are part of a larger community and that we need to nurture our friendships.

The 11th House also represents our hopes and dreams. This is the House of our wishes and aspirations. We all have a vision for our future, and the 11th House reminds us to pursue those dreams. When we align our actions with our intentions, we can make powerful changes in our lives. So, the next time you feel lonely, remember that you have a whole community of friends waiting for you in the 11th House.

The 12th House: House of the Unconscious

The 12th house is often referred to as the "house of the unconscious." This is because it represents the parts of ourselves that we are not usually aware of. This includes our hidden fears, desires, and motivations. The 12th house also represents our karma and past lives. This is why it is sometimes called the "house of self-undoing."

The positive side of the 12th house is that it can help us understand ourselves on a deeper level. By exploring our shadow selves, we can learn to accept and forgive ourselves. We can also gain insights into our past lives and how they are influencing our present situation. However, the 12th house can also be a difficult place to confront our demons. It is important to approach this house with caution and insight, or we may find ourselves lost in its depths.

Extra Geomantic Houses

In addition to the 12 astrological houses, there are also three geomantic houses. These are the houses of the two witnesses and the judge. These houses are used to further understand the chart as a whole. The two witnesses represent the opposing forces at work in

the chart, while the judge represents the outcome.

The Two Witnesses

The two witnesses are traditionally represented by the Sun and Moon. They represent the two opposing forces at work in the chart. The Sun represents our conscious mind, while the Moon represents our unconscious mind. These two forces are always in conflict with each other. The Sun wants us to take action and pursue our goals, while the Moon wants us to stay safe and comfortable. This conflict is what makes us human.

The 1st Witness: House of Beginning

The 1st Witness is associated with the beginning of anything, which makes it an important part of any geomantic reading. This house represents all that is new, fresh, and exciting. It is a time of potential and possibility when anything seems possible. The 1st Witness encourages us to take risks and to venture into the unknown. It is a time of exploration and adventure when we are open to new experiences.

This house reminds us that every journey begins with a single step and that even the smallest act can have significance. So, whatever you are embarking on, remember that the 1st Witness is with you, urging you to take that first step into the great unknown.

The 2nd Witness: House of Progress

The 2nd Witness is associated with progress and forward momentum. This house represents our ability to move forward in life and to make progress towards our goals. It is a time of growth and expansion when we are expanding our horizons. The 2nd Witness reminds us that even when things are tough, we can always find a way to move forward. This house is a reminder that we are never stuck in one place and that there is always room for growth.

This house is a reminder that even when we feel lost, we can always find our way again. So, if you are feeling lost, remember that the 2nd Witness is with you, urging you to keep moving forward.

The Judge: House of Conclusion

The Judge is associated with conclusion and resolution. This house represents our ability to bring things to a close. It is a time of endings and closure when we can let go of the past. The Judge reminds us that even though things may end, there is always something new waiting for us around the corner. This house serves as a reminder that even when things seem dark, there is always a light at the end of the tunnel. So, if you are feeling down, remember that the Judge is with you, urging you to keep going.

The geomantic houses are a fundamental part of any geomantic reading. They provide insight into the various forces at work in the chart and how they interact with each other. By understanding these houses, we can gain a better understanding of our own lives and the world around us.

The houses are divided into 12 astrological houses and three extra geomantic houses. The houses are classified into three groups, the angular houses, the succedent houses, and the cadent houses. The angular houses are the 1st, 4th, 7th, and 10th houses. The succedent houses are the 2nd, 5th, 8th, and 11th houses. The cadent houses are the 3rd, 6th, 9th, and 12th houses.

The astrological houses represent the various areas of our lives, while the extra geomantic houses represent the opposing forces at work in the chart and the outcome. The houses are a reminder that we are constantly moving forward and that there is always room for growth. So, whatever you are going through, remember that the houses are with you, urging you to keep moving forward.

Chapter 5: Preparing Your Mind

To interpret the messages that come to you through geomancy, it is crucial to have a clear mind. The symbols that appear in a geomantic reading can be open to interpretation, and it is important to be able to see them clearly to find the meaning that is most relevant to you.

It's important to have a clear mind with geomancy.
https://pixabay.com/es/photos/hombre-ma%c3%b1ana-amanecer-sentado-2264051/

If your mind is cluttered with worries or distractions, it will be difficult to find the clarity you need. To get the most out of a geomantic reading, take some time beforehand to clear your mind and focus on what you hope to learn. By taking this step, you will be setting yourself up for success.

This chapter will give you some ideas and tips for how to prepare beforehand so that you can get the most out of your geomancy readings.

Preparing for Geomancy

There are many different ways to prepare for a geomancy session, but the most important thing is to make sure that you are comfortable and relaxed. You may want to sit or lie down in a quiet place where you will not be disturbed. You may also want to spend a few minutes meditating or doing some other form of relaxation exercise to clear your mind.

Once you are ready, you can begin to focus on your breath and the energy of the earth. Allow yourself to sink into the ground and become one with the earth's energy. Once you feel connected, you can start to explore the different ways you can use this energy to improve your life.

Here are some steps you can take to prepare for a geomancy session:

1. Clearing Your Mind

The first step is to clear your mind. Over time, our subconscious mind accumulates a lot of mental clutter, and it can be helpful to take some time to declutter before starting a geomancy session. You can do this by focusing on your breath and observing every thought that comes into your mind without judgment. Once you have become more aware of your thoughts, you can start to let go of the ones that are no longer serving you.

Carrying the baggage from your past will only weigh you down and make it difficult to move forward. Take some time to release any thoughts or emotions you have not dealt with yet. If you need help, there are many resources available that can guide you through the process of clearing your mind. Do not leave this step until the last minute. It can take some time to achieve a state of mental

clarity.

2. Connecting with the Earth

It is important to first establish a connection with the Earth to prepare for a geomantic reading. This can be done in many ways, but one simple method is to sit or stand barefoot outside on the ground for a few minutes. As you focus on your breath, feel the Earth's grounding energy entering your body through your feet. Place your hands directly on the ground or hold a piece of raw crystal in each hand.

There are many different ways to work with natural elements to prepare for a geomancy reading. One simple method is to spend time outside in nature, paying attention to the patterns around you. Notice how the leaves blow in the wind, the branches grow on trees, and the water flows in a river. These patterns can offer guidance and insight into your life.

Once you feel connected to the Earth, you can begin to still your mind and open yourself up to receive guidance from the natural world around you. Trust that the answers you seek will be revealed to you through the patterns of the rocks, trees, and other elements in the landscape. You may also want to ask the Earth for help in understanding the messages you receive.

3. Developing Your Intuition

Geomancers work with the land to connect with its spirit and bring about positive change. To become a geomancer, it is essential to develop your intuition. Intuition is a form of knowing the things that go beyond the five senses. It is a way of accessing knowledge that is not available through logical reasoning.

There are many different ways to develop your intuition. One simple method is to spend time each day practicing meditation or mindfulness. As you focus on your breath and still your mind, you will begin to notice the subtle thoughts and feelings that arise. With practice, you will be able to quiet your mind and focus more easily on your intuition.

To develop your intuition, begin by spending time in nature. Connect with the earth beneath your feet and heed the guidance that comes into your heart. You may also find it useful to work with a mentor who can help you hone your skills. With practice, you will

develop the ability to read the earth's energy and use it to bring about positive change.

You can also develop your intuition by paying attention to your dreams. Keep a dream journal and write down the details of your dreams as soon as you wake up. Over time, you will begin to notice patterns and symbols that mean something to you. These messages can offer guidance and insight into your life.

4. Protecting Yourself Spiritually

Anyone interested in pursuing geomantic readings should take some time to prepare themselves spiritually. This means creating a safe space where you can focus on your reading without any outside distractions. It also means being aware of your energy and how it might affect the reading.

One simple way to protect yourself spiritually is to create an altar. An altar can be as simple or as elaborate as you like. It can be a dedicated space in your home or a portable box you take with you when traveling. Fill your altar with items that represent your intention for the reading. You might include crystals, herbs, photos, or symbols that have meaning for you.

Another way to protect yourself spiritually is to cleanse your energy before you begin. This can be done with a salt bath, by smudging with sage, or by using any other method you feel drawn to. The important thing is to cleanse your space and yourself so that you can approach the reading with a clear mind.

You may also want to meditate or do some other type of relaxation exercise to clear your mind and open yourself up to the experience. And finally, it is important to set an intention for the reading. What do you hope to learn? What are you looking for guidance on? By taking some time to prepare mentally and emotionally, you will be able to get the most out of your geomantic reading.

5. Doing Daily Exercises

You can do a few exercises every day to help you on your journey to becoming a geomancer. By taking time each day to focus on your breath and connect with your body, you will start to develop a deeper understanding of your energy field. This will be helpful when it comes time to read the energy of a space or person.

Daily exercises will help ground and center you, making it easier to receive clear information during readings. They will also protect you from outside influences that can disrupt your reading. Make sure to set aside some time each day to focus on your practice. If you are unsure where to start, plenty of resources are available online or in your local library.

6. Noticing Recurring Patterns

As you work with geomancy, you will start noticing patterns in the world around you. It is vital to become attuned to recurring patterns in both the physical and abstract worlds. By doing this, you will be able to easily find the symbols that will give you information about the issue at hand.

To begin, take some time each day to notice the patterns around you, both in your immediate environment and in the larger world. Pay attention to how the light falls on objects, how shadows are cast, and how people and animals move through space. As you become more attuned to these patterns, you will start to see them everywhere, providing you with a wealth of information to work with during your readings.

Meditation Exercises

Meditation plays an important role in the practice of geomancy. Through meditation, you will develop a deeper understanding of your energy and how it interacts with the world around you. There are many different ways to meditate, so find a method that works for you and stick with it. Here are a few basic exercises to get you started.

1. Grounding Meditation

This meditation is designed to help you connect with the earth and ground your energy. It is a simple exercise that can be done anywhere, at any time. We must first ground ourselves in meditation to read the earth's energy. This will help us to clear our minds and open our hearts to the earth's wisdom.

To begin, find a comfortable place to sit or lie down. Close your eyes and take a few deep breaths. Imagine roots growing from your feet, connecting you to the earth's center. Feel the earth's energy entering your body, filling you with strength and grounding you in

your power. Allow yourself to be still, at peace, and receptive to the earth's guidance. When you are ready, open your eyes and begin your reading.

2. Intuition Meditation

This meditation is designed to help you connect with your intuition and the unseen world. It will allow you to access the knowledge and guidance available to you. The exercise is simple, but it may take some time to master. Be patient with yourself and trust that you will receive the information you need.

To begin, find a comfortable place to sit or lie down in. Close your eyes and take a few deep breaths. Imagine yourself surrounded by a bright, white light. This light is filled with wisdom and knowledge and is here to guide you. Allow yourself to relax and receive the light's guidance. When you are ready, open your eyes and begin your reading.

3. Visualization

One of the most important steps in preparing for geomantic readings is to learn how to visualize. This skill is essential for reading the patterns formed by the lines and shapes in the sand. The ability to clearly see these patterns will allow you to interpret them more easily and make more accurate readings. With practice, it will become second nature, and you will be able to do it without even thinking.

To develop your visualization skills, find a quiet place where you can comfortably sit or lie down. Close your eyes and take a few deep breaths. Begin to picture the lines and shapes in your mind's eye. As you become more comfortable with visualization, you will be able to see the patterns clearly. With practice, you will be able to interpret the meaning of these patterns and use them to make predictions.

4. Mantras

Mantras are sacred syllables or phrases used as a tool for meditation. When recited correctly, mantras can help focus the mind and promote feelings of peace and well-being. For those new to mantra meditation, finding one that really resonates with you can be helpful. Once you have chosen a mantra, it is important to recite it correctly.

The correct pronunciation of mantras is said to be essential for unlocking their power. Many mantras are recorded so they can be easily and accurately learned. In addition to correct pronunciation, it is also important to recite mantras with intention. Repeat your mantra slowly and mindfully, letting the sound wash over you and fill you with positive energy. With regular practice, you will develop a deeper understanding of mantras' role in geomantic readings.

5. Mudras

Mudras are an important part of geomantic readings. They are gestures used to channel energy and focus the mind. There are many different mudras, and each has its meaning and purpose. Learning about the different mudras and how to use them is important to prepare for a geomantic reading.

The first step is to find a comfortable position. Sit with your spine straight and your legs crossed. Place your hands on your knees, palm up. Take a few deep breaths and close your eyes. Once you are settled, begin by holding the mudra for focus. Place your thumb and index finger together and extend the other fingers. Hold this mudra in front of your third eye, just above the bridge of your nose. Focus on your breath and allow your mind to become still.

Once you have achieved inner peace, you can begin the reading. Remember to keep your mind focused and open to receiving guidance from the universe. Mudras will help you to connect with the energy around you and receive accurate insights.

6. Affirmations

To get the most accurate and helpful readings, it is crucial to be mentally and emotionally prepared. One way to do this is through the use of affirmations. An affirmation is a positive statement that you repeat to yourself to program your mind for success. For example, you might say to yourself, "I am open to all the insight and guidance that the Universe has to offer."

By affirming your intention to receive guidance, you are opening yourself up to the possibility of having a successful reading. Another affirmation that you can use is "I am willing to release all fears and doubts that are holding me back." This affirmation will clear your mind and allow you to receive more fully the messages you are meant to receive.

Repeating these affirmations (or ones like them) before your reading will help to ensure that you are in the right mindset to receive accurate and helpful guidance. The better prepared you are, the more helpful your reading will be.

7. Crystals and Stones

If you are interested in having a geomantic reading done, there are a few things you can do to prepare. One of the most important things is to choose the right crystals and stones. Each type of crystal has its unique properties and energies, so it is important to choose ones that will be supportive of your specific situation.

For example, if you are looking for guidance on your career path, you might choose crystals like citrine or carnelian. If you are hoping to improve your health, you might choose crystals like amethyst or jade. And if you are seeking protection from negative energy, you might choose crystals like black tourmaline or obsidian.

By taking the time to choose the right crystals, you can ensure that your reading is both accurate and helpful. The use of crystals and stones is a powerful way to connect with the energies of the earth and receive guidance from the universe.

8. Candles

Another way to prepare for a geomantic reading is to use candles. Candles are often used in readings because they can create a peaceful and relaxing environment. They can also focus your mind and connect you with the energies of the universe.

When choosing candles for your reading, choosing ones made from natural materials like beeswax or soy is important. You should also choose candles that are scented with essential oils, as these can improve your mood and focus. If you are not sure which candles to choose, you can ask your geomancer for guidance.

The use of candles is a simple but effective way to prepare for a geomantic reading. By choosing the right candles, you can help ensure that your reading is accurate and helpful.

9. Smudging

Smudging is another way to prepare for a geomantic reading. Smudging is the practice of burning herbs and using the smoke to cleanse and purify your space. This is usually done with a bundle of dried sage, but other herbs can also be used. You can also use an

essential oil diffuser or burn candles scented with cleansing oils like eucalyptus or lemon.

Many people find that smudging helps to create a more peaceful and relaxing environment. It is a powerful way to cleanse your space and prepare for a reading. It helps to clear away any negative energy that might be present, and it also helps to focus your mind and connect you with the energies of the universe.

Smudging is a simple but effective way to prepare for a geomantic reading. Taking the time to smudge your area can guarantee that your reading is correct.

10. Protection Ritual

Before your reading, it is also essential to do a protection ritual. This will protect you from any negative energy that might be present. It is crucial to create a space that is sacred and safe. There are many different ways to do this, but one simple method is to cleanse the space with sage smoke. You can also use crystals or other objects to create a circle of protection.

Once your space is ready, you can begin the reading. It is important to relax and clear your mind so that you can receive messages from the universe. Trust your intuition and allow the symbols to guide you. With preparation and an open mind, you will be able to receive the guidance you need from the natural world.

Preparing your mind for a geomantic reading is essential for receiving accurate and helpful guidance. Clearing your mind and opening yourself up to the messages of the universe will ensure that your reading is correct.

There are many different ways to prepare for a reading, but some simple methods include going out in nature, meditating, doing daily exercises, noticing recurring patterns, protecting yourself spiritually, and using candles, crystals, and smudging.

This chapter has given you a few ideas and tips for how to prepare beforehand. The meditation exercises and protection rituals at the end of this chapter will also help you get started. Remember, the most important thing is to relax and trust your intuition. With preparation and an open mind, you will be able to receive the guidance you need from the natural world.

Chapter 6: Casting the Points

Doing a geomantic reading is a lot like reading tea leaves. Geomancy uses markings in the dirt, lines, points, and dots to create figures that are then interpreted. The first step when doing a geomantic reading is casting the points. A variety of methods can be used to do this, from writing the lines randomly to throwing dice, flipping coins, or using geomancy cards.

As the lines, points, and dots are randomly placed, you can use any method. While there are many ways to cast the points, it is vital to personalize the process according to your own beliefs. This chapter will explore the various methods for casting the points and some dos and don'ts to keep in mind while doing so.

The First Step: Casting the Points

The process of casting the points is meant to create random figures that can then be interpreted for their meaning. In some cases, the points may be read directly, while in other cases, they may be used to create more complex geomantic figures. Although the interpretation of geomantic figures can be complex, the process of casting the points is relatively simple and can be done by anyone with just a bit of practice.

When casting the points, the first step is to choose a method. Various methods can be used, from writing the lines randomly to throwing dice, flipping coins, or using geomancy cards. Once a method has been chosen, the points can be cast by following the

instructions for that particular method.

Whether you are looking for guidance on a personal issue or advice on a major life decision, no question is too big or small for geomancy. The only limit is your imagination.

Various Methods for Casting the Points

There are a variety of methods that can be used to cast the points. Some methods are more complex than others, but all can be used to create random figures that can then be interpreted.

1. Writing the Lines Randomly

One of the simplest methods for casting the points is to randomly draw lines randomly. This method involves drawing a series of lines, points, and dots on a piece of paper or another surface. The lines, points, and dots can be drawn in any order and with any amount of space between them. Once the lines, points, and dots have been drawn, they can be interpreted for their meaning.

When using this method, ensure that the lines, points, and dots are randomly placed. To personalize this method, you can use a randomly generated word or phrase as a guide for where to place the lines, points, and dots.

2. Throwing Dice

Dice can also be used to cast the points. This method involves rolling a pair of dice and using the numbers you get to determine where to place the lines, points, and dots. This can be done with two regular six-sided dice or with four special geomantic dice.

Throwing dice is sometimes used to cast the points.
https://pixabay.com/es/photos/costa-rica-dado-dice-dados-dices-4979191/

The color of the dice can also be used to add meaning to the figures that are created. White dice represent purity, while black dice represent darkness. Red dice represent passion, while blue dice represent calm. Green dice represent growth, while yellow dice represent wisdom.

To begin, the dice are thrown onto a flat surface. The dots on the dice represent the elements of fire, water, air, and earth. The total of the dots determines which element is being represented. For example, if the total is 12, then the element would be fire. Once the element has been determined, it can be entered into the chart.

The numbers on the dice can be interpreted in various ways, but one common method is to use the numbers as coordinates. This means that the first number rolled corresponds to the x-coordinate, and the second number rolled corresponds to the y-coordinate. This method of casting points is quick and easy; anyone can learn how to do it!

3. Flipping Coins

Flipping coins is another method for casting points.
https://unsplash.com/photos/b4D7FKAghoE?utm_source=unsplash&utm_medium=referr
al&utm_content=creditShareLink

Flipping coins is another popular method for casting points. This can be done with a regular coin, or you can use a special geomantic coin. Once you have your coin, you will need to decide how many

points you want to cast. Each point represents a different aspect of your question, and the more points you cast, the more detailed your reading will be.

To cast your points, simply flip your coin onto the ground and observe which way it lands. Heads are considered positive, while tails are negative. You can interpret the results in various ways, but one common method is to use the positions of the coins to create a geomantic figure. This figure can then be interpreted for its meaning.

4. Using Geomancy Cards

Geomancy cards are a special deck of cards used for divination. Each card in the deck represents a different element, and the deck can be used to cast the points. To use the geomancy cards, simply shuffle the deck and lay out the cards in a row. The number of cards in your layout will depend on how many points you want to cast.

Once the cards are laid out, interpret their meaning based on the traditional meanings of the elements. For example, fire is associated with passion, while water is associated with emotions. Use the card positions to create a geomantic figure, and then interpret the figure for its meaning.

The printables at the end of this book can be used to create your geomantic cards. Simply print out the sheets, cut out the cards, and then shuffle them.

5. Casting the Points with a Pendulum

A pendulum can also be used to cast the points. This method involves holding a pendulum over a piece of paper or other surface and allowing it to swing freely. This method is quick and easy, and anyone can learn how to do it. The only downside is that it can be difficult to interpret the results. You can use various Pendulums for this method, but one common type is a quartz crystal Pendulum.

To use this method, simply hold the pendulum over the paper or surface. The pendulum will swing in a variety of directions. Take note of the direction it swings and the number of times it swings. This will give you the coordinates for where to place the lines, points, and dots. Once all of the coordinates have been determined, you can interpret the figure for its meaning.

6. Casting the Points with a Bowl of Water

The traditional way of casting points for geomantic readings is to use a bowl of water. The bowl is filled with water and placed on a table or other flat surface. The querent then stirs the water with their finger while concentrating on their question. After a minute or so of stirring the water, they remove their finger and look at the pattern made by the ripples.

The pattern interpretation is based on the specific shapes that are formed and the overall balance of positive and negative space. The space around the querent's finger is considered positive, while the space away from the finger is considered negative.

If there is more positive space, then the reading is considered favorable. However, the reading is interpreted as unfavorable if there is more negative space. This method is quick and easy, and anyone can learn how to do it.

7. Casting the Points with a Flame

Another traditional method for casting points is to use a flame. This method involves lighting a candle and then allowing the wax to drip into a bowl of water. The querent then concentrates on their question while the wax is melting. Once the wax has melted, the querent looks at the pattern that is formed and interprets it for its meaning.

This method is similar to the water method but uses a flame instead of water. The interpretation is based on the same principles, but using a flame can add an extra layer of meaning. For example, fire is associated with passion, so a reading that features a lot of fire energy may be interpreted as being passionate or intense.

The specific shapes formed by the wax can also be interpreted for their meaning. For instance, a heart shape may represent love, while a spiral shape may represent transformation. If you are using this method, it is crucial to be familiar with the traditional meanings of the shapes.

8. Casting the Points with Stones

Stones can also be used to cast the points. This method involves placing a stone on each of the geomantic figures. The querent then concentrates on their question while holding the stones. Based on the stones' positions, the querent can interpret the figure for its

meaning. This method can be used with any type of stone, but some common choices include quartz crystals, amethysts, and rose quartz.

The stones can be placed on the figures in a variety of ways. The most common method is to place them in the center of each figure. However, they can also be placed on the lines that connect the figures. The interpretation will be based on the stones' positions and energies.

If you are using this method, selecting stones that are energetically compatible with the question you are asking is vital. For example, if you are asking a question about love, you would want to choose stones that are associated with love, such as rose quartz or amethyst.

9. Casting the Points Using Sticks

One of the simplest and most effective ways to cast points for a reading is to use sticks. First, find a clearing in nature where you will be undisturbed. Then, collect a bundle of small sticks and find a comfortable place to sit. Close your eyes and take a few deep breaths, letting go of all your worries and concerns.

Open your eyes and cast the sticks onto the ground when you are ready. The patterns that they make can be interpreted according to traditional geomantic meanings. For example, a row of four sticks pointing in the same direction may represent growth or new beginnings.

This method is great for connecting with nature and tapping into your intuition. It is also one of the easiest methods to learn since there is no need to memorize complex shapes or symbols. By taking the time to connect with the Earth through geomancy, you can gain valuable insights into your life journey.

10. Casting the Points with a Deck of Cards

You can also use a regular deck of playing cards to cast the points. This complex method requires knowledge of the traditional meanings of the geomantic figures. There are many different ways to do this, but one of the most common is to deal four cards for each figure.

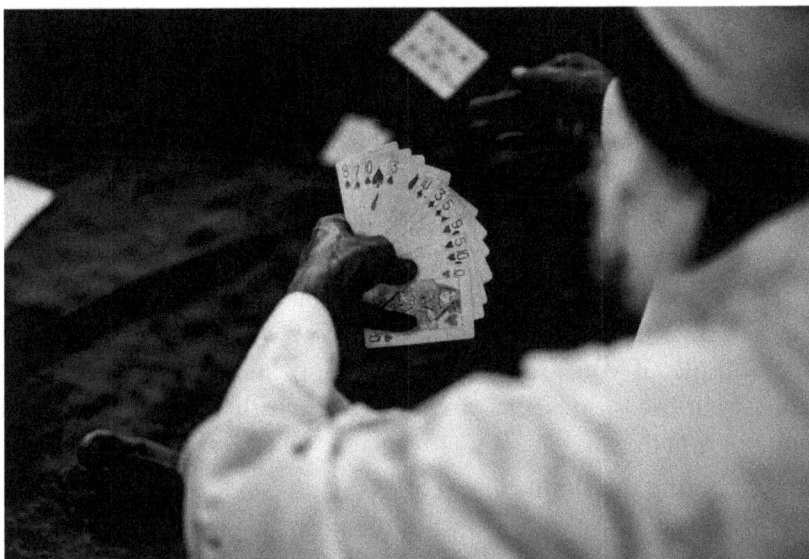

A basic set of playing cards can be used to cast points.
https://pixabay.com/es/photos/adulto-asia-tarjetas-divertida-3170055/

The specific position of the cards will determine the meaning of the figure. For example, if the first card is placed in the center of the figure, it will represent the querent. The other three cards will represent the influences of the past, present, and future.

To begin, shuffle the deck of cards and then deal out four cards face down. These four cards represent the four geomantic figures. Next, deal out four more cards and place them on top of the first four. Then, deal out four more cards and place them on top of the second set of four. The querent then asks their question.

The final step is to turn over the cards and interpret the figures based on the traditional meanings. This method can be quite complex, but it can be used for any question, especially for those relating to the querent's past, present, and future. By understanding the influences of each period, the querent can gain valuable insights into their life journey.

Personalizing the Method

While there are many ways to cast the points, the critical part is to find a method that works for you. If you are new to geomancy, it is best to start with a simple method and then build up to more complex ones. Some simple methods include using sticks or stones.

If you want to personalize the method, you can use objects that are significant to you. For example, if you are asking a question about your career, you could use coins or shells. The key is choosing objects that you feel comfortable with and that have personal meaning.

As you become more familiar with geomancy, you can experiment with different methods and techniques. You can move on to more complex methods, such as using a deck of cards. Or you can try different ways of interpreting the figures. There is no right or wrong way to do it. Finding a method that works for you and one you feel comfortable with is important.

Do's and Don'ts of Casting the Points

Geomantic reading is a personal experience, so there are no hard and fast rules about how to cast the points. However, there are a few things to remember to ensure you get the most out of your reading.

Do

- Find a quiet place where you will not be disturbed
- Relax and take a few deep breaths before you begin
- Choose a method you feel comfortable with
- Ask a specific question. The more specific the question, the more accurate the reading will be
- Be open to the answers you receive

Do Not

- Rush through the process
- Force the figures to fit your question
- Be afraid to ask tough questions

By following these simple guidelines, you can ensure that you get the most out of your geomantic reading. While these are just the basic things, here are some extra tips:

A. Asking the Question

The first step is to ask a specific question. The more specific the question, the more accurate the reading will be. First, make sure that the question is clear and specific. This will help focus the reading and produce more accurate results. Secondly, do not be too

vague or open-ended. Asking a question like "What does my future hold?" is likely to produce very confusing results. *Be as specific as possible.*

Finally, remember that the question should be framed in a way that can be answered with a yes or no. Asking a question like "Should I move to a new city?" will give you much more useful information than asking, "What are my options?" By following these simple guidelines, you can ensure that you get the most accurate reading possible from your geomantic points.

B. Avoiding Mistakes

There are a few common mistakes people make when doing geomancy readings. The first mistake that is made is rushing through the process. Secondly, they try to force the figures to fit their question. Thirdly, they are afraid to ask tough questions. By avoiding these mistakes, you can ensure that you get the most accurate reading possible.

If you find that you are making these mistakes, do not worry. Just take a step back and relax. Remember, there is no rush. Take your time and focus on your question. Then, let the figures fall where they may. The most important thing is to be open to the answers you receive.

C. Interpreting the Figures

Once you have cast the points, it is time to interpret the figures, and there are a few different ways to do this. First, you can look up the meaning of each figure in a book or online. Second, you can ask someone else to interpret the figures for you. Finally, you can interpret the figures yourself.

If you choose to interpret the figures yourself, there are a few things to keep in mind. First, trust your intuition. Second, look at the overall pattern of the figures. Third, pay attention to any recurring themes. By following these simple guidelines, you can ensure that you get the most accurate reading possible.

D. Other Tips and Advice

Here are a few other tips and pieces of advice to keep in mind when doing geomancy readings.

- Do not be afraid to experiment. There is no one right way.

- Do not be afraid to ask tough questions and be open to the answers you receive.

- Trust your intuition and keep an open mind.

- Keep a journal of your readings. This will help you track your progress and see how your skills develop over time.

- Do not take the readings too seriously. Remember, they are just a tool to help you gain insights into your life. They are not always 100% accurate.

- Geomancy is a great way to connect with your intuition and gain insights into your life. Enjoy the process and see what insights you can glean from it.

Casting the points is the first step in doing a geomancy reading. This chapter discussed the various methods of casting the points, as well as how to avoid common mistakes. For beginners, it is recommended to use the traditional methods of casting the points using colored dice, sticks, or coins.

When you are confident with your skills, you can start to experiment with other methods of casting the points. It is important to be specific in your question, open to the answers you receive, and avoid mistakes such as rushing through the process.

After casting the points, you can then interpret the figures. There are a few different ways to interpret the figures, including looking up the meaning of each figure, asking someone else to interpret the figures, or interpreting the figures yourself. The next chapter will discuss how to interpret the figures in more detail.

So, there you have it, a complete guide on how to cast the points for a geomancy reading. By following these simple tips, you can ensure that you get the most accurate reading possible.

Chapter 7: The Geomantic Figures

Can the same be said about geomantic figures? What do they mean, and is there more than one way to interpret them?

Once you have learned how to cast the points and create the geomantic figures, you will want to understand their meaning. The symbols used in geomancy are based on ancient ideas about the four elements, the planets, and the zodiac.

Each figure has its meaning, and you can gain insights into your own life and situation by interpreting the figures. In addition, geomancy can be used for divination or predicting the future. By asking a question and casting the points, you can receive guidance from the geomantic figures.

With practice, you will develop your ability to interpret the symbols and use them to gain insights into your life path. This chapter will provide an introduction to the meanings of the geomantic figures.

Decrypting Geomantic Figures

Geomantic figures are created by making marks in the sand or dirt. The number of marks and the way they are arranged all have meaning. For example, a figure with four marks arranged in a cross shape indicates that the person is feeling balanced and stable. A

figure with eight marks arranged in a circle indicates that the person is feeling connected to their surroundings.

We can learn a lot about individuals' inner lives by decoding the meaning of these graphs. In some cultures, geomantic figures are used for divination to help people make decisions about their future. In other cultures, they are used as part of healing rituals, providing a way for people to express their fears and anxieties. Regardless of how they are used, geomantic figures offer a valuable window into the human soul.

What They Mean

Geomantic figures can be divided into two groups. The first group includes the four elemental figures, representing matter's fundamental building blocks. The second group includes the twelve zodiacal figures, representing the energies that shape our lives.

Geomancy uses the arrangement of 16 figures, each composed of four points. Of these, eight are considered "positive" or "active," and the other eight are "negative" or "passive." The active figures are those in which the first and third points are both marked, while the passive figures are those in which only the second and fourth points are marked.

The eight active figures are called "masculine," while the eight passive figures are called "feminine." The masculine figures represent the Yang energy, while the feminine figures represent the Yin energy. These energies are believed to be in constant interaction, and the interplay between them creates the universe's harmony.

The Connection between Figures

Here are some things that connect the four types of geomantic figures:

1. Elements

There are four main types of geomantic figures, water, fire, earth, and air. Each type has its unique characteristics, but they also have some things in common. All four types of figures are associated with a specific element. Water figures are associated with the element of water, fire figures with the element of fire, earth figures with the element of earth, and air figures with the element of air.

2. Zodiac Signs

The 12 zodiac figures are each associated with a specific zodiac sign. Water signs are associated with the signs of Cancer, Scorpio, fire signs are associated with the signs of Aries, Leo, and Sagittarius, earth signs are associated with the signs of Taurus, Virgo, and Capricorn, and air signs are associated with the signs of Gemini, Libra, and Aquarius.

3. Planets

All four types of figures are connected to a specific planet. Water figures are connected to the planet Mercury, fire figures are connected to the planet Mars, earth figures are connected to the planet Saturn, and air figures are connected to the planet Jupiter. The connection between planets and geomantic figures can help us understand these astronomical bodies' influence on our lives.

4. Divination

Finally, all four types of figures have a specific role in divination. Water figures represent emotions and intuition, fire figures represent passion and energy, earth figures represent stability and structure, and air figures represent intellect and wisdom. By understanding these commonalities, you can begin to see how each type of figure is related to the others.

Understanding the Properties of the Figures

If you want to learn more about the geomantic figures, it is crucial to understand the properties of each type. Here is a brief overview of the properties of geomantic figures:

1. **Quality:** A figure can be stable or mobile. A stable figure does not change, while a mobile figure is in flux. The stability or mobility of a figure reflects the quality of the energy it represents.

2. **Direction:** A figure can be entering, exiting, or both. An entering figure is one that is moving towards something, while an existing figure is one that is moving away from something. The direction of a figure reflects the flow of energy it represents.

3. **Humor:** A figure can be sanguine, choleric, melancholy, and phlegmatic. Sanguine humor is associated with positive

emotions like happiness and optimism, choleric humor with negative emotions like anger and frustration, melancholy humor with introspection and contemplation, and phlegmatic humor with apathy and indifference.

4. **A Measure of Time:** A figure can be associated with a specific moment in time. The time associated with a figure reflects the duration of the energy it represents. The longer the time frame, the more significant the figure.

5. **Partiality:** A figure can be partial or impartial. A partial figure is one that applies to a specific situation, while an impartial figure is one that can be applied to any situation. The partiality of a figure reflects the specific nature of the energy it represents.

By understanding the properties of geomantic figures, you can begin to see how they can be used in divination.

Interpreting the Figures

Now that you have a basic understanding of the geomantic figures, it is time to learn how to interpret them. When interpreting the figures, it is crucial to keep the following guidelines in mind:

1. **The Position of the Figure in Relation to the Others**: The position of a figure can tell you a lot about its meaning. For example, a figure in the center of the chart is considered to be more important than the ones on the periphery.

2. **The Orientation of the Figure:** The orientation of a figure can also be important. An upright figure is considered more positive than a reversed one.

3. **The Type of Figure:** The type of figure can help understand its meaning. For example, a water figure is typically associated with emotions, while a fire figure is typically associated with passion.

4. **The Planet Associated with the Figure:** The planet associated with a figure can also help you understand its meaning. For example, a figure associated with the planet Mercury is typically associated with communication and commerce.

The General Meaning of Each Figure

Now that you know how to interpret the figures, it is time to learn about their meanings. Here is a brief overview of the general meaning of each figure:

Tristitia

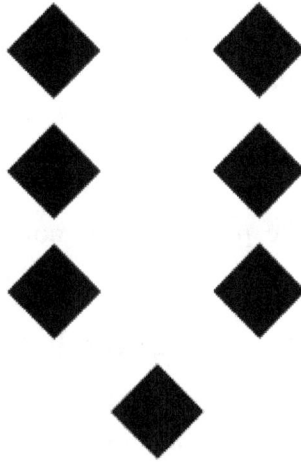

Trisitia.
https://commons.wikimedia.org/wiki/File:Geomantic_tristitia.svg

Translation: Sorrow

Keywords: Loss, Grief, Sadness, Depression

Ruling Element: Earth

Ruling Planet: Saturn

Ruling Zodiac Sign: Aquarius

Quality: Stable

Direction: Entering

Partial/Impartial: Partial

Diurnal/Nocturnal: Diurnal

Tristitia is a figure associated with loss and grief. It can represent a sad or depressing situation. It can also indicate a period of transition or change. This figure is typically associated with the planet Saturn and the zodiac sign Aquarius. The quality of Tristitia is stable, which represents the constancy of emotions like sadness

and grief.

The direction of this figure is entering, which means that it is moving towards something. This could represent the beginning of a period of grief or the start of a new chapter in life. The partiality of this figure indicates that it only applies to specific situations. This figure is diurnal, which means that it is active during the day.

Puer

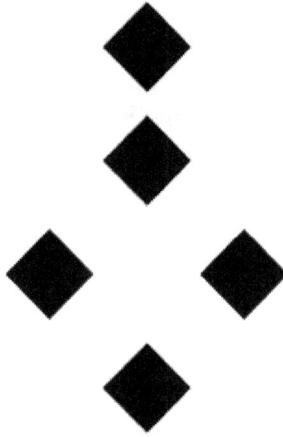

Puer.

Translation: Boy

Keywords: Youth, Innocence, Beginnings

Ruling Element: Air

Ruling Planet: Mars

Ruling Zodiac Sign: Aries

Quality: Mobile

Direction: Exiting

Partial/Impartial: Partial

Diurnal/Nocturnal: Diurnal

Puer is a figure associated with youth and innocence. It can represent the beginning of a new project or venture. It can also indicate a time of growth or expansion. This figure is typically associated with the planet Mars and the zodiac sign Aries. The quality of Puer is mobile, which represents the energy and activity of youth.

The direction of this figure is exiting, which means it is moving away from something. This could represent the end of a project or the completion of a phase of growth. The partiality of this figure indicates that it only applies to specific situations. This figure is diurnal, which means that it is active during the day.

Rubeus

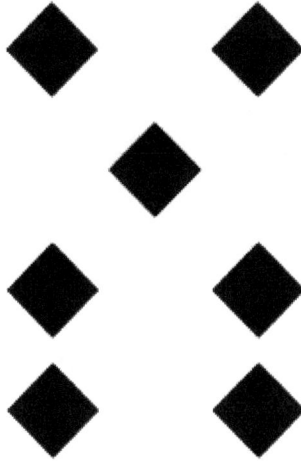

Rubeus.

Translation: Red

Keywords: Anger, Aggression, Violence, Passion

Ruling Element: Air

Ruling Planet: Mars

Ruling Zodiac Sign: Scorpio

Quality: Mobile

Direction: Exiting

Partial/Impartial: Partial

Diurnal/Nocturnal: Nocturnal

Rubeus is a figure associated with anger and aggression. It can represent a violent or passionate situation. It can also indicate a time of upheaval or change. This figure is typically associated with the planet Mars and the zodiac sign Scorpio. The quality of Rubeus is mobile, which represents the energy and activity of anger.

The direction of this figure is exiting, which means it is moving away from something. This could represent the end of a situation or the completion of a phase of change. The partiality of this figure indicates that it only applies to specific situations. This figure is nocturnal, which means it is active during the night.

Caput Draconis

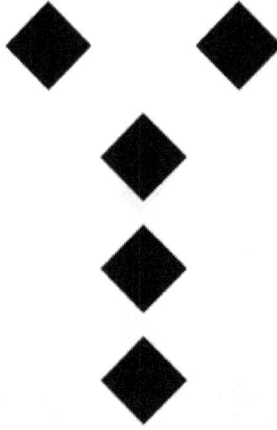

Caput draconis.
https://commons.wikimedia.org/wiki/File:Geomantic_caputdraconis.svg

Translation: Dragon's Head

Keywords: Transformation, New Beginnings, Metamorphosis

Ruling Element: Earth

Ruling Planet: Moon's North Node

Ruling Zodiac Sign: Pisces

Quality: Stable

Direction: Entering

Partial/Impartial: Partial

Diurnal/Nocturnal: Diurnal

Caput Draconis is a figure associated with transformation and new beginnings. It can represent a changing or evolving situation. It can also indicate a time of growth or expansion. This figure is typically associated with the Lunar Nodes and the zodiac sign Pisces. The quality of Caput Draconis is stable, which represents the constancy of change.

The direction of this figure is entering, which means it is moving towards something. This could represent the beginning of a new phase or the start of a new chapter in life. The partiality of this figure indicates that it only applies to specific situations. This figure is diurnal, which means it is active during the day.

Cauda Draconis

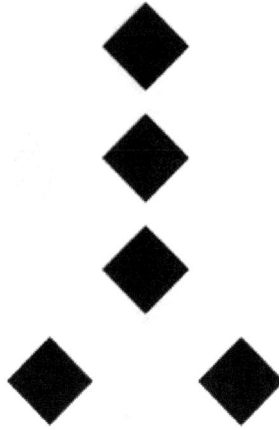

Cauda Draconis.

Translation: Dragon's Tail

Keywords: Endings, Completion, Death

Ruling Element: Fire

Ruling Planet: Moon's South Node

Ruling Zodiac Sign: Virgo

Quality: Mobile

Direction: Exiting

Partial/Impartial: Partial

Diurnal/Nocturnal: Nocturnal

Cauda Draconis is a figure associated with endings and completion. It can also represent death, but that is not always the case. The fire element rules this figure which represents passion and intensity. The planet associated with Cauda Draconis is the Moon's South Node, which is a point of karma and destiny.

The ruling zodiac sign is Virgo, an earth sign associated with service and practicality. This figure is mobile, meaning that it is constantly changing and is never in one place for long. It is also partial, which means that it is not complete and always has the potential to change. Cauda Draconis is a nocturnal figure, meaning that it is most powerful at night.

Puella

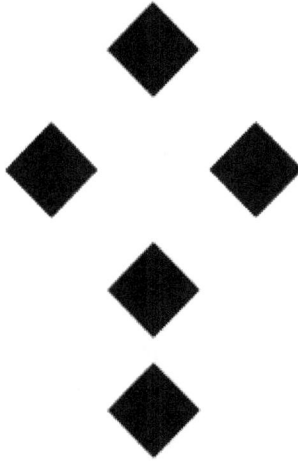

Puella.

Translation: Girl

Keywords: Youth, Innocence, Beginnings

Ruling Element: Water

Ruling Planet: Venus

Ruling Zodiac Sign: Libra

Quality: Stable

Direction: Entering

Partial/Impartial: Partial

Diurnal/Nocturnal: Diurnal

Puella is a figure that represents youth and innocence. It can also signify beginnings, as it is associated with the water element, which is representative of new beginnings. The planet Venus rules this figure, which is associated with love, beauty, and femininity. The zodiac sign Libra is also ruled by Venus and is symbolized by the scales of justice.

Puella is a stable figure, meaning that it does not change much over time. It is also partial, indicating that there is always room for growth and development. This figure is diurnal, meaning that it is most powerful during the day.

Conjunctio

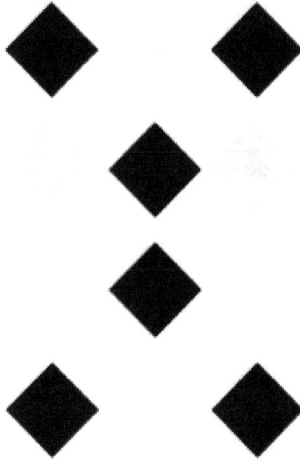

Conjunctio.
https://commons.wikimedia.org/wiki/File:Geomantic_conjunctio.svg

Translation: Union

Keywords: Partnership, Cooperation, Balance

Ruling Element: Air

Ruling Planet: Mercury

Ruling Zodiac Sign: Gemini

Quality: Mobile

Direction: Both

Partial/Impartial: Impartial

Diurnal/Nocturnal: Nocturnal

Conjunctio is a figure that represents partnership and cooperation. It is also associated with the air element, which signifies balance. The planet Mercury rules this figure, which is associated with communication and commerce. This figure is mobile, meaning that it is constantly changing and never in one place for long. It is also impartial, which means that it does not favor one side over the other. Conjunctio is a nocturnal figure, meaning that it is most powerful at night.

Albus

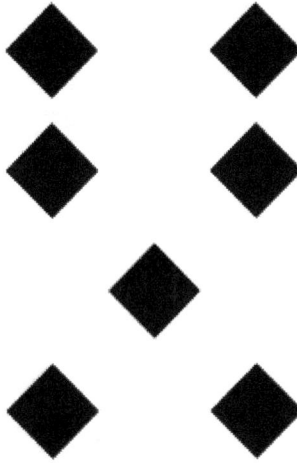

Albus.
https://commons.wikimedia.org/wiki/File:Geomantic_albus.svg

Translation: White

Keywords: Purity, Hope, New Beginnings

Ruling Element: Water

Ruling Planet: Mercury

Ruling Zodiac Sign: Gemini

Quality: Stable

Direction: Entering

Partial/Impartial: Partial

Diurnal/Nocturnal: Diurnal

Albus is a figure that represents purity and hope. It is also associated with the water element, which signifies new beginnings. The planet Mercury rules this figure, which is associated with communication and commerce. This figure is stable, meaning that it does not change much over time. It is also partial, indicating that there is always room for growth and development. Albus is a diurnal figure, meaning that it is most powerful during the day.

Via

Via.

Translation: Road

Keywords: Journey, Change, Movement

Ruling Element: Earth

Ruling Planet: Moon

Ruling Zodiac Sign: Cancer

Quality: Mobile

Direction: Both

Partial/Impartial: Impartial

Diurnal/Nocturnal: Nocturnal

Via is a figure that represents journey and change. It is also associated with the earth element, which signifies stability. The planet Moon rules this figure, which is associated with emotions and intuition. This figure is mobile, meaning that it is constantly changing and never in one place for long. It is also impartial, which means that it does not favor one side over the other. Via is a nocturnal figure, meaning that it is most powerful at night.

Populus

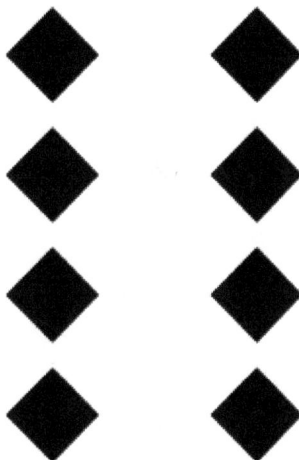

Populus.
https://commons.wikimedia.org/wiki/File:Geomantic_populus.svg

Translation: People

Keywords: Community, Society, Relationship

Ruling Element: Water

Ruling Planet: Moon

Ruling Zodiac Sign: Aquarius

Quality: Stable

Direction: Both

Partial/Impartial: Impartial

Diurnal/Nocturnal: Diurnal

Populus is a figure that represents community and society. It is also associated with the water element, which signifies relationships. The planet Moon rules this figure, which is associated with emotions and intuition. This figure is stable, meaning that it does not change much over time. It is also impartial, which means that it does not favor one side over the other. Populus is a diurnal figure, meaning that it is at its most powerful during the day.

Fortuna Minor

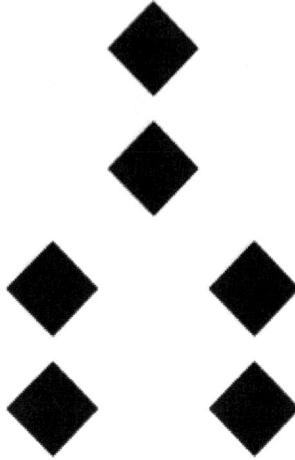

Fortuna minor.
https://commons.wikimedia.org/wiki/File:Geomantic_fortunaminor.svg

Translation: Lesser Fortune

Keywords: Opportunity, Good Luck, Progress

Ruling Element: Fire

Ruling Planet: Sun

Ruling Zodiac Sign: Leo

Quality: Mobile

Direction: Exiting

Partial/Impartial: Impartial

Diurnal/Nocturnal: Diurnal

Fortuna Minor is a figure that represents opportunity and good luck. It is also associated with the fire element, which signifies progress. The planet Sun rules this figure, which is associated with vitality and life force. This figure is mobile, meaning it is constantly changing and never in one place for long. It is also impartial, which means that it does not favor one side over the other. Fortuna Minor is a diurnal figure, meaning that it is most powerful during the day.

Acquisitio

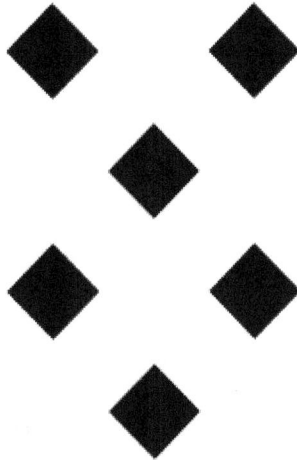

Acquisito.
https://commons.wikimedia.org/wiki/File:Geomantic_acquisitio.svg

Translation: Acquisition

Keywords: Gain, Profit, Success

Ruling Element: Air

Ruling Planet: Jupiter

Ruling Zodiac Sign: Sagittarius

Quality: Stable

Direction: Entering

Partial/Impartial: Impartial

Diurnal/Nocturnal: Diurnal

Acquisitio is a figure that represents gain and success. It is also associated with the air element, which signifies expansion. The planet Jupiter rules this figure, which is associated with abundance and prosperity. This figure is stable, meaning that it does not change much over time. It is also impartial, which means that it does not favor one side over the other. Acquisitio is a diurnal figure, meaning that it is most powerful during the day.

Amissio

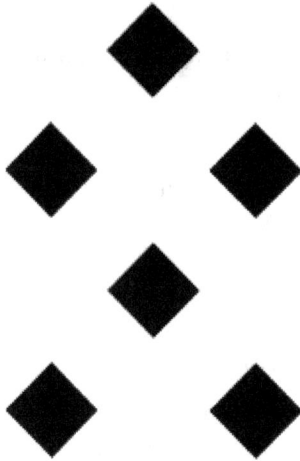

Amissio.
https://commons.wikimedia.org/wiki/File:Geomantic_amissio.svg

Translation: Loss

Keywords: Defeat, Setback, Failure

Ruling Element: Fire

Ruling Planet: Venus

Ruling Zodiac Sign: Capricorn

Quality: Mobile

Direction: Exiting

Partial/Impartial: Impartial

Diurnal/Nocturnal: Nocturnal

Amissio is a figure that represents loss and failure. It is also associated with the fire element, which signifies destruction. The planet Venus rules this figure, which is associated with love and beauty. This figure is mobile, meaning that it is constantly changing and never in one place for long. It is also impartial, which means that it does not favor one side over the other. Amissio is a nocturnal figure, meaning that it is most powerful at night.

Cancer

Translation: Prison

Keywords: Restriction, Delay, Frustration

Ruling Element: Earth

Ruling Planet: Saturn

Ruling Zodiac Sign: Capricorn

Quality: Stable

Direction: Both

Partial/Impartial: Impartial

Diurnal/Nocturnal: Nocturnal

Carcer is a figure that represents restriction and delay. It is also associated with the earth element, which signifies stability. The planet Saturn rules this figure, which is associated with limitations and boundaries. This figure is stable, meaning that it does not change much over time. It is also impartial, which means that it does not favor one side over the other. Carcer is a nocturnal figure, meaning that it is most powerful at night.

Fortuna Major

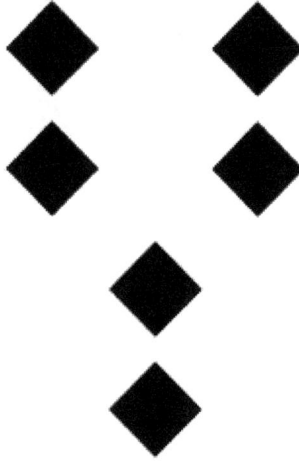

Fortuna major.

Translation: Greater Fortune

Keywords: Good Luck, Success, Progress

Ruling Element: Earth

Ruling Planet: Sun

Ruling Zodiac Sign: Leo

Quality: Stable

Direction: Entering

Partial/Impartial: Impartial

Diurnal/Nocturnal: Nocturnal

Fortuna Major is a figure that represents good luck and success. It is also associated with the earth element, which signifies grounding. The planet Sun rules this figure, which is associated with vitality and life force. This figure is stable, meaning that it does not change much over time. It is also impartial, which means that it does not favor one side over the other. Fortuna Major is a nocturnal figure, meaning that it is most powerful at night.

Laetitia

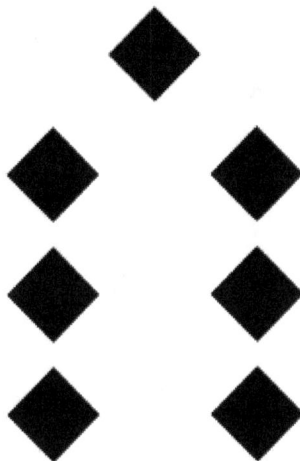

Laetitia.

Translation: Joy

Keywords: Happiness, Celebration, Triumph

Ruling Element: Fire

Ruling Planet: Jupiter

Ruling Zodiac Sign: Pisces

Quality: Mobile

Direction: Exiting

Partial/Impartial: Partial

Diurnal/Nocturnal: Nocturnal

Laetitia is a figure that represents happiness and celebration. It is also associated with the fire element, which signifies passion. The planet Jupiter rules this figure, which is associated with luck and opportunity. This figure is mobile, meaning that it is constantly changing and never in one place for long. It is also partial, which means that it favors one side over the other. Laetitia is a nocturnal figure, meaning that it is most powerful at night.

Interpreting the Geomantic Figures can give you a greater understanding of the energies at play in your life. They can also help you make decisions by providing guidance and insight. To

learn more about the Geomantic Figures, consult a professional astrologer or tarot reader. This chapter only scratches the surface of this complex and fascinating topic.

Note: No figure is purely negative, and the reader should not perceive any figure as a bad omen.

Chapter 8: Constructing a Shield Chart

Do you easily see signs and understand them? Do you feel as if you have a strong connection to the spiritual world? If your answer is yes, then it is time for you to start learning how to practice geomancy. Once you have cast your geomantic figures, it is time to construct a shield chart to start the interpretation process.

The shield chart is the main structure through which you can do a geomantic reading. This step is vital to understanding the message your figures are trying to tell you. In this chapter, we will discuss the shield chart in detail, including its segments and what each of them represents. By the end of this chapter, you will know how to construct your shield chart and interpret its message.

The Geomantic Shield Chart

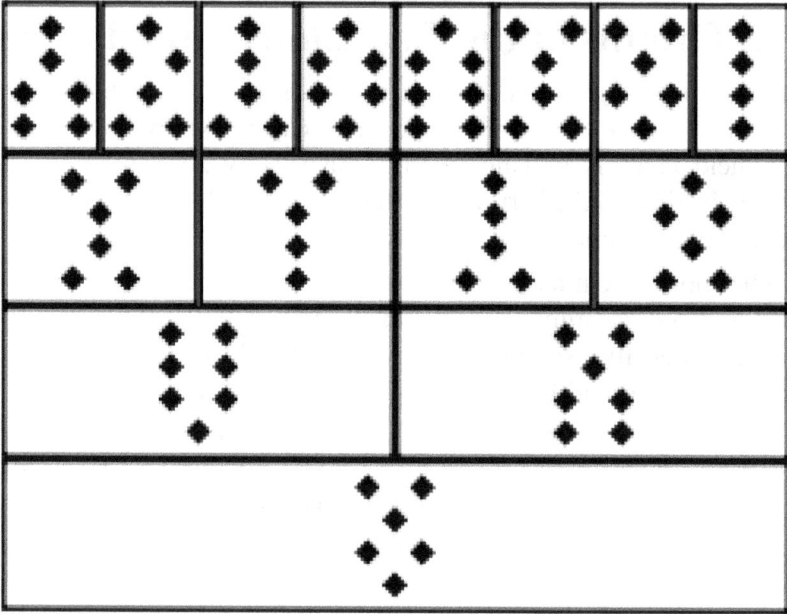

The geomantic shield chart.

https://commons.wikimedia.org/wiki/File:Geomantic_shieldchart.svg

The geomantic shield is the primary tool used to interpret a geomantic reading. The shield chart is made up of 16 house segments, each of which corresponds to a specific geomantic figure. These house segments are further divided into 4 groups of 4 houses each, called quadrants. The quadrants are used to delineate the different areas of a person's life that the reading may be touching on.

The shield chart is read from the bottom up. The first quadrant, which is the bottommost one, corresponds to the most recent past. The second quadrant corresponds to the near future. The third quadrant corresponds to the distant future, and the fourth quadrant, the topmost one, corresponds to the outcome.

The quadrants are not equal in size, nor are the house segments within each quadrant. The size and placement of the quadrants and house segments are all determined by the specific question you are asking or the topic of your reading. The shield chart can be used for a variety of purposes, such as answering specific questions, doing

general readings, or understanding the energy of a particular situation.

The Origins of the Geomantic Shield Chart

The origins of the shield chart are unknown, but it is believed to have originated in the Arab world. The earliest known mention of the shield chart is in Fate of the Universe by Abu al-Rayhan al-Biruni. In this book, Biruni describes a shield chart that is used to predict future events.

This book includes a description of how to construct a shield chart and the meaning of each quadrant and house segment. It is believed that the shield chart was later adopted by European geomancers, who added their twists and modifications.

Some people believe that the geomantic shield chart originated in China, where it was used as a tool for divination. Feng Shui practitioners believe that the chart can be used to identify areas of imbalance in a space and to make recommendations for correcting those imbalances.

The use of the geomantic shield chart has spread to other parts of Asia and has also gained popularity in the West. Today, there are many different versions of the chart, each of which has its unique symbols and meaning. In the next section, we will take a closer look at the function of the geomantic shield chart.

The Function of the Geomantic Shield Chart

A geomantic shield chart is a tool used by Feng Shui practitioners to evaluate the energy of a space. The shield chart is used to interpret the message of the geomantic figures. The figure that falls in each housing segment can give you information about the past, present, and future. When you are doing a reading for yourself, you will need to construct your geomantic shield chart.

To help you better understand the shield chart, here are some of its functions:

- The geomantic shield chart can be used to answer specific questions

- It can be used to get a general overview of a situation
- It can be used to understand the energy of a particular situation
- It can be used to make recommendations for improving the energy of a space
- It can be used to find areas of imbalance in a space
- It can be used to understand the dynamics of a relationship
- It can be used to make predictions

Having a better understanding of the geomantic shield chart will help you to use it more effectively. In the next section, we will take a closer look at the segments of a geomantic shield chart.

The Segments of the Geomantic Shield Chart

The geomantic shield chart is composed of four segments, each representing a different stage in the reading process. The first segment, known as the Mothers, is used to identify the potential influences on a given situation. The second segment, the Daughters, is used to further refine the reading by considering the nature of the influences at play.

The third segment, the Witnesses, is used to weigh the evidence and determine which course of action is best. Finally, the fourth segment, the Judge, is used to pronounce a verdict based on the findings of the previous three segments. By carefully considering all four segments, practitioners can gain a deeper understanding of the complex interplay between human and natural forces.

The following section will provide you with a more detailed look at each of the segments in a geomantic shield chart.

A. The Mothers

Description: The first segment of the chart, known as the Mothers, is used to identify the potential influences on a given situation. This segment is divided into four quadrants, each of which is ruled by a different Mother. These Mothers represent the four elements of fire, earth, air, and water.

Each Mother has a unique symbol and meaning. The Mothers can be used to understand the energy of a space and to make recommendations for improving the balance of that space. The Mothers are the fundamental forces at work in any given situation, and they can be either positive or negative.

Meaning: The Mothers represent the building blocks of reading, and they can be thought of as the foundation upon which the rest of the chart is built. The Mothers provide the reader with a starting point from which they can understand the situation at hand. The first step in any reading is to identify the Mother that is most relevant to the question at hand.

This Mother will provide the reader with an initial understanding of the situation and will give them a general idea of what to expect. From there, the reader can begin to refine their understanding by considering the other Mothers.

What Each Figure Transmits in a Reading

When a geomantic figure is sitting in the Mother's shield segment, it is transmitting a very important message. For example, if the figure is 'Puella,' then it is transmitting a message of purity, innocence, and new beginnings. If the figure is 'Populus,' then it is transmitting a message of community, cooperation, and compromise.

Similarly, Fortuna Major is associated with good fortune, luck, and opportunity. When sitting in the Mother's shield segment, it can indicate that the situation is favorable. Via is associated with passion, enthusiasm, and energy. When used within the Mother's shield segment, it can indicate that the issue at hand is of great importance.

The Mothers segment of the chart is used to identify the potential influences on a given situation.

B. The Daughters

Description: The second segment of the chart, known as the Daughters, is used to further refine the reading by considering the nature of the influences at play. This segment is divided into four quadrants, each of which is ruled by a different Daughter. These Daughters represent the four suits of the tarot, cups, swords, wands, and pentacles.

Each Daughter has a unique symbol and meaning. The Daughters can be used to understand the dynamics of a situation and to make recommendations for how to best navigate that situation. The Daughters are the more specific forces at work in any given situation, and they can be either positive or negative.

Meaning: The Daughters provide the reader with a more specific understanding of the situation at hand. The second step in any reading is to identify the Daughter that is most relevant to the question at hand. This Daughter will provide the reader with an idea of what to expect. From there, the reader can begin to refine their understanding by considering the other Daughters.

What Each Figure Transmits in a Reading

When a geomantic figure is sitting in the Daughter's shield segment, it means that the figure is specifically transmitting a message about that suit. For example, if the figure is 'Rubeus,' then it is transmitting a message about the suit of wands (fire). This message could be interpreted to mean that the situation is dangerous or that caution should be exercised.

If the figure is 'Cauda Draconis,' then it is transmitting a message about the suit of swords (air). This message could be interpreted to mean that the situation is confused or that there is a need for clarification. The Daughters segment of the chart is used to understand the specific influences at work in any given situation.

C. The Witnesses

Description: The third segment of the chart, known as the Witnesses, is used to further refine the reading by considering the role that other people play in the situation. This segment is divided into four quadrants, each of which is ruled by a different Witness. These Witnesses represent the four elements: fire, air, water, and earth.

Each Witness has its unique symbol and meaning. The Witnesses can be used to understand the dynamics of a situation and to make recommendations for how to best navigate that situation. The Witnesses are the people or factors that are not directly involved in the situation, but that can still have an impact on it.

Meaning: The Witnesses provide the reader with a more specific understanding of the situation at hand. The third step in any reading is to identify the Witness that is most relevant to the question at hand. This Witness will provide the reader with an idea of what to expect. From there, the reader can begin to refine their understanding by considering the other Witnesses.

What Each Figure Transmits in a Reading

When a geomantic figure is sitting in the Witness's shield segment, it means that the figure is specifically transmitting a message about that element. For example, if the figure is 'Albus,' then it is transmitting a message about the element of water. This message could be interpreted to mean that the situation is emotional or that there is a need for sensitivity.

If the figure is 'Populus,' then it is transmitting a message about the element of earth. This message could be interpreted to mean that the situation is materialistic or that there is a need for practicality. The Witnesses segment of the chart is used to understand the people or factors that are not directly involved in the situation, but that can still have an impact on it.

D. The Judge

Description: The fourth and final segment of the chart is known as the Judge. This segment is used to determine the outcome of the reading. The Judge is represented by a single geomantic figure, which is placed in the center of the chart. This figure is known as the 'Judge' because it represents the final decision that will be made in the situation.

The Judge is not influenced by the other segments of the chart; instead, its determination is based on the position of the planets and the stars. The Judge is considered impartial and objective, and as such, their decision is final.

Meaning: The Judge provides the reader with a definitive understanding of the outcome of the situation. The fourth and final step in any reading is to identify the Judge. This graph will tell the reader what to anticipate. The Judge is not influenced by the other segments of the chart but makes its determination based on the position of the planets and the stars.

What Each Figure Transmits in a Reading

When a geomantic figure is sitting in the Judge's shield segment, it means that the figure is specifically transmitting a message about that planet or star. For example, if the figure is 'Fortuna Major,' then it is transmitting a message about the planet Jupiter. This message could be interpreted to mean that the situation will have a positive outcome.

If the figure is 'Via,' then it is transmitting a message about the star Saturn. This message could be interpreted to mean that the situation will have a negative or difficult outcome. The Judge segment of the chart is used to determine the outcome of the reading.

Constructing Your Shield Chart

When constructing a geomancy shield chart, the first step is to identify the question you want to be answered. Once you have done this, you will need to select a location for the chart. The chart can be drawn on any surface, but it is recommended that you use a piece of paper or cloth.

The next step is to identify the Shield Figures that you will use in your chart. There are a total of 16 Shield Figures, and each one represents a different element. You can choose to use all 16 figures, or you can select a smaller number. It is recommended that you select at least 8 figures.

Once you have selected your Shield Figures, you will need to place them in the appropriate segments of the chart. The Shield Figures are placed in the following order:

1. The Significator
2. The Mother
3. The Father
4. The Left Witness
5. The Right Witness
6. The Judge

Once you have placed all of the Shield Figures in their proper positions, you will need to draw lines connecting them. These lines are known as 'shield lines,' and they serve to create a connection

---

between the figures.

Once you have drawn all of the shield lines, you will need to interpret the chart. The interpretation of the chart will depend on the question that you have asked, as well as the Shield Figures that you have used.

Putting It into Practice: Printable Shields

Now that you know how to construct a geomancy shield chart, you can put your knowledge into practice. At the end of the book are printable shields you can use for your readings. Use these shields to answer a question you have, and see what the outcome will be.

This chapter has provided you with a detailed explanation of how to construct a geomancy shield chart. You have also learned how to interpret the results of your chart. Constructing one is a simple process that anyone can do. All you need is a question, a location, and 16 Shield Figures. Once you have these things, you can construct your chart and begin to interpret the results. Try it for yourself and see what the future has in store for you.

Chapter 9: Generating an Astrological Chart

Do you know what your astrological chart looks like? If not, do not worry! In this chapter, we will show you how to generate an astrological chart so that you can begin to understand the role that astrology plays in your life. Geomancy and astrology are inextricably linked. A deep understanding of one will enhance your understanding of the other.

This chapter will explore how to use and interpret the second most common chart used by geomancers, the astrological chart. We will go through each house and explain what changed and the specific meaning each geomantic figure might transmit if situated in each of the astrological houses. But first, we need to understand what an astrological chart is.

Astrological Charts

An astrological chart is a snapshot of the sky at the moment you were born. It shows the position of the planets at that moment, as well as the signs of the zodiac in which they appear. An astrological chart is a two-dimensional map of the heavens at a specific moment in time. It is composed of twelve houses, each representing a different area of life experience, and ten planets, each representing different astrological energy.

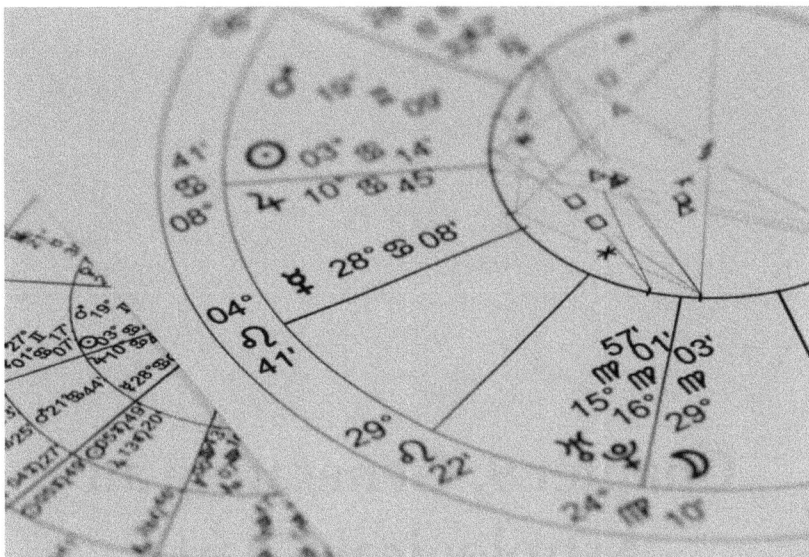

Astrological chart.

CC0 Public Domain https://pxhere.com/en/photo/682841

In addition, the chart includes the two nodes of the Moon, Rahu and Ketu, as well as the four angles of the chart, the Ascendant, Descendant, Midheaven, and IC (or Imum Coeli). These are the most important points in the chart, as they indicate the beginning, ending, highest point, and lowest point of your journey through life, respectively.

Planets in an Astrological Chart

The planets in an astrological chart are Sun, Moon, Mercury, Venus, Mars, Jupiter, Saturn, Uranus, Neptune, and Pluto. Each planet represents a different type of energy, which manifests in different ways in our lives. The Sun, for example, represents our ego and our sense of self. The Moon represents our emotions and our subconscious mind.

Mercury represents our communication style, and Venus represents our values and what we find beautiful. Mars represents our drive and ambition, and Jupiter represents our luck and expansion. Saturn represents our lessons and limitations, and Uranus represents our freedom and individuality. Neptune represents our spirituality and connection to the divine, and Pluto represents our power and transformation.

The Astrological Houses

The twelve houses of the astrological chart represent different areas of life experience. A geomantic figure situated in a particular house will have a different meaning than if it were in another house. Based on the planet that rules the house and the sign that occupies the said house, its meaning will change.

Understanding the meaning of the astrological houses is essential to understanding the role astrology plays in your life. This section will provide an overview of how a geomantic figure might be interpreted if situated in each of the twelve houses.

House of Self

Keywords: Self-identity, physical appearance, first impressions

The geomantic figure in the 1st House has a strong influence on your outward appearance and how you are seen by others. This figure is associated with your physical body and how you present yourself to the world. It also relates to your overall health and well-being.

If the figure is well-aspected, it indicates that you are likely both physically healthy and appealing. If the figure is poorly-aspected, it suggests that you may have physical health problems or an unattractive appearance. Whether well or poorly aspected, the 1st House figure is an important indicator of how you will be perceived by others.

When interpreting a figure in the 1st House, it is important to pay attention to the element and quality of the figure, as well as the planet that rules it. This will give you clues as to how the figure will manifest in your appearance and health.

For example, a Fire element figure in the 1st House indicates that you likely have a fiery personality and that you are very self-assertive. A Water element figure in the 1st House suggests that you are likely emotionally sensitive and that you have a compassionate nature.

House of Possessions

The geomantic figure in the 2nd House has a strong influence on your material possessions and your financial wellbeing. This figure is associated with your income, possessions, and values. It also

---

relates to your self-esteem and your sense of self-worth.

If the figure is well-aspected, it indicates that you are likely financially successful and that you have high self-esteem. If the figure is poorly-aspected, it suggests that you may have financial problems or low self-esteem. Either way, the 2nd House figure is an important indicator of your relationship with money and possessions.

When interpreting a figure in the 2nd House, it is important to pay attention to the element and quality of the figure, as well as the planet that rules it. This will give you clues as to how the figure will manifest in your finances and possessions.

For example, a Fire element figure in the 2nd House indicates that you are likely generous with your money and possessions. A Water element figure in the 2nd House suggests that you are likely stingy with your money and possessions.

House of Communications

The geomantic figure in the 3rd House has a strong influence on your communication style and your ability to express yourself. This figure is associated with your verbal and written communication, as well as your ability to think clearly and reason logically. It also relates to your mental health and overall state of mind.

If the figure is well-aspected, it indicates that you are likely to articulate and that you have a sharp mind. If the figure is poorly-aspected, it suggests that you may have communication problems or mental health issues. Either way, the 3rd House figure is an important indicator of your ability to express yourself and engage in intellectual pursuits.

When interpreting a figure in the 3rd House, it is important to pay attention to the element and quality of the figure, as well as the planet that rules it. This will give you clues as to how the figure will manifest in your communication and thought processes. For example, a Fire element figure in the 3rd House indicates that you are likely expressive and enthusiastic when communicating. A Water element figure in the 3rd House suggests that you are likely introspective and compassionate when you are communicating.

House of Home and Family

The geomantic figure in the 4th House strongly influences your home life and family relationships. This figure is associated with your family, your ancestors, and your sense of belonging. It also relates to your emotional well-being and your overall state of mind.

If the figure is well-aspected, it indicates that you likely have a happy home life and a close relationship with your family. If the figure is poorly-aspected, it suggests that you may have problems with your family or your emotional health. Either way, the 4th House figure is an important indicator of your relationship with your home and family.

When interpreting a figure in the 4th House, it is important to pay attention to the element and quality of the figure, as well as the planet that rules it. This will give you clues as to how the figure will manifest in your home life and family relationships. For example, a Fire element figure in the 4th House indicates that you are likely passionate and fiery in your relationships with your family. A Water element figure in the 4th House suggests that you are likely compassionate and introspective in your relationships with your family.

House of Creativity

The geomantic figure in the 5th House strongly influences your creativity and self-expression. This figure is associated with your hobbies, creative projects, and love life. It also relates to your sense of fun and your overall state of mind.

If the figure is well-aspected, it indicates that you are likely creative and that you have an active love life. If the figure is poorly-aspected, it suggests that you may have problems with your creative endeavors or your love life. Either way, the 5th House figure is an important indicator of your ability to express yourself creatively and enjoy romantic relationships.

The element and quality of the figure, as well as the planet that rules it, will give you clues as to how the figure will manifest in your creativity and love life. For example, a Fire element figure in the 5th House indicates that you are likely creative and passionate in your hobbies and relationships. A Water element figure in the 5th House suggests that you are likely introspective and compassionate

in your hobbies and relationships.

House of Health and Work

The geomantic figure in the 6th House strongly influences your health and work life. This figure is associated with your physical health, daily routine, and job. It also relates to your mental health and your overall state of mind.

If the figure is well-aspected, it indicates that you likely have good physical and mental health. If the figure is poorly-aspected, it suggests that you may have problems with your health or your work life. Either way, the 6th House figure is an important indicator of your ability to maintain a healthy lifestyle and to be productive when it comes to your work.

The element and quality of the figure, as well as the planet that rules it, will give you clues as to how the figure will manifest in your health and work life. For example, a Fire element figure in the 6th House indicates that you are likely passionate and fiery in your approach to work and health. A Water element figure in the 6th House suggests that you are likely introspective and compassionate in your approach to work and health.

House of Balance

The geomantic figure in the 7th House strongly influences your relationships and interactions with others. This figure is associated with your close relationships, your marriage, and your business partnerships. It also relates to your sense of fair play and your overall state of mind.

If the figure is well-aspected, it indicates that you likely have harmonious relationships with others. If the figure is poorly-aspected, it suggests that you may have problems with your relationships or your sense of fair play. The 7th House figure is an important indicator of your ability to interact with others positively.

The element and quality of the figure, as well as the planet that rules it, will give you clues as to how the figure will manifest in your relationships with others. For example, a Fire element figure in the 7th House indicates that you are likely passionate and fiery in your interactions with others. A Water element figure in the 7th House suggests that you are likely introspective and compassionate in your interactions with others.

House of Transformation

The geomantic figure in the 8th House has a strong influence on your transformation and rebirth. This figure is associated with your death, your taxes, and your sex life. It also relates to your ability to let go of the past and move on to new beginnings.

If the figure is well-aspected, it indicates that you likely have a positive transformation in your life. If the figure is poorly-aspected, it suggests that you may have problems with your ability to let go of the past or move on to new beginnings. The 8th House figure is an important indicator of your ability to change and grow.

The element and quality of the figure, as well as the planet that rules it, will give you clues as to how the figure will manifest in your transformation and rebirth. For example, a Fire element figure in the 8th House indicates that you are likely to be passionate and fiery in your approach to change and growth. A Water element figure in the 8th House suggests that you are likely introspective and compassionate in your approach to change and growth.

House of Higher Learning

The geomantic figure in the 9th House strongly influences your higher learning and spiritual knowledge. This figure is associated with your higher education, your philosophy, and your religion. It also relates to your ability to see the big picture and find meaning in life.

If the figure is well-aspected, it indicates that you likely have a positive experience with higher learning and spiritual knowledge. If the figure is poorly-aspected, it suggests that you may have problems with your ability to see the big picture or find meaning in life. The 9th House figure is an important indicator of your ability to learn and grow spiritually.

The element and quality of the figure, as well as the planet that rules it, will give you clues as to how the figure will manifest in your higher learning and spiritual knowledge. For example, a Fire element figure in the 9th House indicates that you are likely passionate and fiery in your approach to higher learning and spirituality. A Water element figure in the 9th House suggests that you are likely introspective and compassionate in your approach to higher learning and spirituality.

House of Career

The geomantic figure in the 10th House has a strong influence on your career and public reputation. This figure is associated with your profession, your status, and your achievements. It also relates to your ability to be successful in the public eye.

If the figure is well-aspected, it indicates that you likely have a positive experience with your career and public reputation. If the figure is poorly-aspected, it suggests that you may have problems with your ability to be successful in the public eye. The 10th House figure is an important indicator of your ability to achieve your goals.

The element and quality of the figure, as well as the planet that rules it, will give you clues as to how the figure will manifest in your career and public reputation. For example, a Fire element figure in the 10th House indicates that you are likely passionate and fiery in your approach to your career and public image. A Water element figure in the 10th House suggests that you are likely introspective and compassionate in your approach to your career and public image.

House of Friendships

The geomantic figure in the 11th House has a strong influence on your friendships and social interactions. This figure is associated with your friends, your allies, and your community. It also relates to your ability to connect with others and form meaningful relationships.

If the figure is well-aspected, it indicates that you likely have positive experiences with friendships and social interactions. If the figure is poorly-aspected, it suggests that you may have problems with your ability to connect with others or form meaningful relationships. The 11th House figure is an important indicator of your ability to build strong social bonds.

The element and quality of the figure, as well as the planet that rules it, will give you clues as to how the figure will manifest in your friendships and social interactions. For example, a Fire element figure in the 11th House indicates that you are likely passionate and fiery in your approach to friendships and socializing. A Water element figure in the 11th House suggests that you are likely introspective and compassionate in your approach to friendships

and socializing.

House of the Unconscious

The geomantic figure in the 12th House strongly influences your unconscious mind and your spiritual journey. This figure is associated with your subconscious, your dreams, and your mysticism. It also relates to your ability to connect with the spiritual realm.

If the figure is well-aspected, it indicates that you likely have positive experiences with your unconscious mind and your spiritual journey. If the figure is poorly-aspected, it suggests that you may have problems with your ability to connect with the spiritual realm or access your subconscious mind. The 12th House figure is an important indicator of your ability to connect with the unseen world.

The element and quality of the figure, as well as the planet that rules it, will give you clues as to how the figure will manifest in your unconscious mind and spiritual journey. For example, a Fire element figure in the 12th House indicates that you are likely passionate and fiery in your approach to your unconscious mind and spirituality. A Water element figure in the 12th House suggests that you are likely introspective and compassionate in your approach to your unconscious mind and spirituality.

The astrological chart is the second most commonly used chart by geomancers. It consists of twelve houses, each representing a different area of life. When interpreting an astrological chart, the geomancer will look at the position of the planets in each house, as well as the aspects between the planets.

The geomancer will look at the elements and qualities of the planets, as well as the rulership of each planet. Each planet and house will have a different meaning, which the geomancer will use to interpret the chart. This chapter has explored how to use and interpret the second most common chart used by geomancers, the astrological chart.

Chapter 10: Methods of Interpretation

Each geomantic chart can be interpreted for various reasons, and looking at specific things might help with the interpretation process. This last chapter will provide various interpretative techniques that will help you look at more aspects of a chart and do more accurate readings.

In this chapter, you will learn how to do a daily, weekly, monthly, or yearly chart, how to do a general life reading both for yourself and someone else (or even for a pet), and how to do a reading to find direction in life or the right career, to find a location, to calculate how much time it takes until something happens and so on.

Various Interpretation Techniques

Many techniques can be used for interpretation, but some are more common than others. In this section, we will look at the most common ones.

1. The Four Pillars

The four pillars technique is the most common and basic. It involves looking at the four main pillars of a chart and interpreting them based on their meaning. The first pillar is the self, which represents the querent or the person who is having the reading

done. The second pillar represents the people and things around the querent. The third pillar is the past, which represents the events and experiences that have led up to the present situation. The fourth pillar is the future, which represents the potential outcomes of the current situation.

2. The Twelve Houses

This is another common technique that involves looking at the twelve houses of a chart and interpreting them based on their meaning. This technique is often used in conjunction with the four pillars technique. Based on the position of the planets in the twelve houses, an astrologer can interpret the chart in many different ways. To refresh your knowledge about the twelve houses, see Chapter 4.

3. The Ten Planets

The ten planets technique is another common technique that involves looking at the ten planets of a chart and interpreting them based on their meaning. The way this technique is used can vary, but often, the planets are divided into two groups of five. The first group is the inner planets, which represent the personal self, and the second group is the outer planets, which represent the social self. The planets are also often divided into three groups, which represent the mind, body, and spirit.

4. The Node Axis

The node axis technique is a more advanced technique that involves looking at the nodes of the moon and interpreting them based on their meaning. The North Node represents the future, while the South Node represents the past. This technique is often used to look at the karma of a person or to see how someone's past life experiences are affecting their current life. It can also be used to look at the potential outcomes of a current situation.

5. The Fixed Stars

The fixed stars technique is a more advanced technique that involves looking at the fixed stars and interpreting them based on their meaning. The fixed stars can give clues about a person's destiny or the outcome of a current situation. The interpretation of fixed stars is often made in conjunction with the node axis technique.

How to Do a Reading

There are many different ways to do a reading, but there are some basic steps common to all readings. This section will look at some of the most common types of readings and how to do them.

1. Daily/ Weekly/ Monthly/ Yearly Charts

The first step in doing a daily, weekly, monthly, or yearly chart is choosing the type of chart you want to use. There are many different types of charts, but the most common are the ones that use the four pillars or the twelve houses. Once you have chosen a chart, you will need to determine the time frame you want to use. For a daily chart, you will need the time, date, and place of birth. For a weekly chart, you will need the time, date, and place of birth, as well as the current week's planetary positions.

For a monthly chart, in addition to the time, date, and place of birth, you will need the current month's planetary positions. This can be done using an ephemeris or an online calculator. Similarly, for a yearly chart, in addition to the time, date, and place of birth, you will need the current year's planetary positions. The best way to get this information is to use ephemeris.

The next step is to plot the planets on the chart. This can be done by hand or by using an online program. Once the planets are plotted, you will need to interpret the chart. The interpretation of the chart will depend on the type of chart you are using. If you are using a four-pillar chart, you will need to interpret the chart based on the meaning of the houses. If you are using a twelve-house chart, you will need to interpret the chart based on the meaning of the planets in each house.

2. General Life Reading

A general life reading is a reading that can be done at any time and does not require a specific time, date, or place of birth. In a general life reading, you will use the planetary positions of the day you are doing the reading. You will also need to know your rising sign, the sign that was rising on the horizon at the time and place of your birth.

The rising sign will give clues about your personality and your overall approach to life. To do a general life reading, you will first

need to choose a chart. The most common chart used for a general life reading is the twelve-house chart. Once you have chosen a chart, you will need to determine your rising sign. This can be done by using an online calculator or an ephemeris.

The interpretation of the chart will depend on the planets in each house and their relationship to the rising sign. The planets will give clues about different areas of your life, such as your career, love life, and family life. The rising sign will give clues about your overall approach to life.

3. Relationship Reading

A relationship reading can be done to examine the dynamics of a current or past relationship. In a relationship reading, you will use the birth data of both partners. You will also need to know the current planetary positions. This can be done by using an ephemeris or an online calculator.

The next step is to choose a chart. The most common chart used for a relationship reading is the composite chart. A composite chart is created by taking the midpoint of each planet between two birth charts. This can be done by hand or by using an online program. Once the composite chart is created, you will need to interpret it.

The interpretation will depend on the planets in each house and their relationship to one another. The planets will give clues about different aspects of the relationship, such as communication, intimacy, and conflict.

4. Career Reading

A career reading is a reading that can be done to examine your current career or to explore potential ones. In a career reading, you will use the planetary positions of the day you are doing the reading. You will also need to know your rising sign, the sign that was rising on the horizon at the time and place of your birth.

The rising sign will give clues about your personality and your overall approach to life. To do a career reading, you will first need to choose a chart. The most common chart used for a career reading is the twelve-house chart. Once you have chosen a chart, you will need to determine your rising sign. This can be done by using an online calculator or by an ephemeris.

The interpretation will depend on the planets in each house and their relationship to the rising sign. The planets will give clues about different areas of your career, such as your work environment, your bosses, and your co-workers. The rising sign will give clues about your overall approach to your career.

5. Reading for Finding a Location

A reading for finding a location can be done to find the ideal place to live or to visit. In reading to find a location, you will use the planetary positions of the day you are doing the reading. You will also need to know your rising sign, the sign that was rising on the horizon at the time and place of your birth.

The rising sign will give clues about your personality and your overall approach to life. To do a reading for finding a location, you will first need to choose a chart. The most common chart used for this is the twelve-house chart. Once you have chosen a chart, you will need to determine your rising sign. This can be done by using an online calculator or an ephemeris.

The interpretation of the chart will depend on the planets in each house and their relationship to the rising sign. The planets will provide clues about different aspects of a location, such as its climate, terrain, and people. The rising sign will give clues about your overall approach to the location.

6. Calculating How Much Time It Takes Until Something Happens

There are a couple of different methods that can be used to calculate how much time it will take until something happens. The first method is to use the planetary hours. To do this, you will need to know the time of day and the planetary positions. This can be done by using an ephemeris or an online calculator. Once you have the time of day and the planetary positions, you will need to calculate the planetary hour for the planet that signifies the event.

The second method is to use the astrological ages. The astrological ages are based on the precession of the equinoxes. To calculate the astrological age, you will need to know the year of your birth and the current year. You will then need to find the planet that is in the same sign as the Sun was in at your time of birth. This planet will be in the same sign for everyone born in your year.

The astrological age will give you a general idea of how long it will take for the event to happen. The planetary hour will give you a more specific time frame.

Tips and Tricks

If you want to read a chart, there are a few things that you should keep in mind.

- Relax and clear your mind before you begin. This will help you be more receptive to the information in the chart.

- Focus on your question. This will help you filter out any irrelevant information to your question.

- Take your time. There is a lot of information in a chart, and it can take some time to process it all.

- Keep an open mind. The interpretation of a chart is not an exact science, and there will always be some room for interpretation.

- Be prepared to read the chart more than once. As you gain experience, you will be able to understand the chart better and see things you missed the first time around.

- Always start with your rising sign. This will give you an idea of your overall approach to the chart.

- Pay attention to the planets in each house and their relationship to the rising sign. The planets will give clues about different areas of your life.

- The aspects between the planets are also important. The aspects will give clues about the relationships between the different areas of your life.

- Pay attention to the Moon. The Moon will give you clues about your emotions and your intuition.

- Remember that a chart is only a tool. It is up to you to interpret it and make decisions about your life.

There are a variety of different ways to interpret a chart. You can use the planets, the houses, the aspects, or the rising sign to get information about different areas of your life. The different charts can be used to get information about specific areas of your life or to

find a location. The astrological ages and the planetary hours can be used to calculate how much time it will take until something happens.

Conclusion

As we have seen, the planets play a vital role in geomancy. They are the building blocks of our universe, and their energies shape our lives and experiences. By understanding the planets and their interactions, we can begin to make sense of the chaos of the cosmos and unlock the secrets of our lives.

The elements and zodiac signs are important concepts in geomancy. They provide a framework for understanding the energies of the cosmos and how they interact with one another. By understanding the elements and zodiac signs, we can develop a greater understanding of ourselves and the world around us.

The geomantic houses are another important tool that can be used to understand the different areas of our lives. Geomancy is an incredibly powerful and insightful tool that can be used to enhance our understanding of astrology.

In the first chapter of this guide, we introduced the basics of geomancy, including its history and how it is used to interpret the energies of the cosmos. In the second chapter, we explored the importance of planets in geomancy and how they can be used to understand our own lives and experiences. The third chapter delved into the elements and zodiac signs and how they interact with one another to create the unique energies of each person.

In the fourth chapter, we learned about the geomantic houses and how they can be used to understand the different areas of our lives. The fifth chapter explored the importance of preparing your

mind for geomancy. The sixth chapter discussed how to cast the points to generate a reading. In the seventh chapter, we looked at the different geomantic figures and how they can be interpreted.

The eighth chapter covered the construction of a shield chart, and in the ninth chapter, we generated an astrological chart. Finally, in the tenth chapter, we explored some methods of interpretation that can be used to make sense of your readings.

Geomancy is a powerful tool that can be used to enhance our understanding of the cosmos and our place within it. By delving into the history, concepts, and methods of this ancient practice, we can develop a greater understanding of ourselves, our experiences, and the world around us.

Here's another book by Mari Silva that you might like

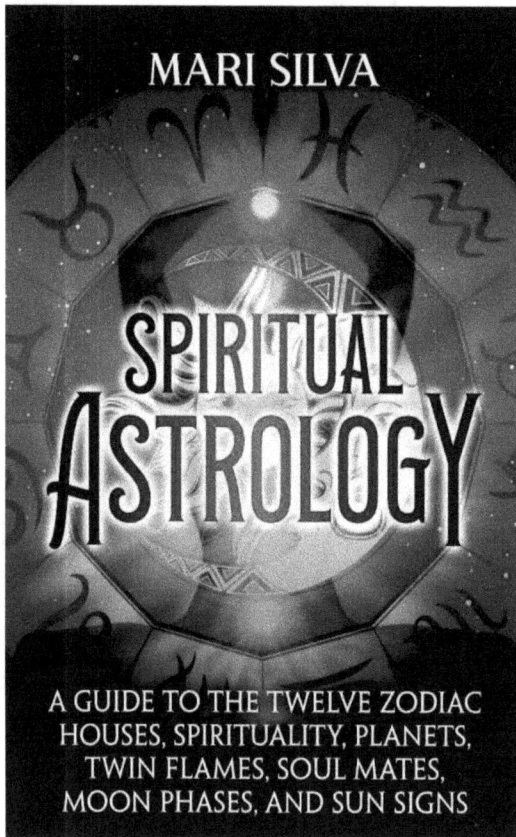

MARI SILVA

SPIRITUAL ASTROLOGY

A GUIDE TO THE TWELVE ZODIAC HOUSES, SPIRITUALITY, PLANETS, TWIN FLAMES, SOUL MATES, MOON PHASES, AND SUN SIGNS

Your Free Gift (only available for a limited time)

Thanks for getting this book! If you want to learn more about various spirituality topics, then join Mari Silva's community and get a free guided meditation MP3 for awakening your third eye. This guided meditation mp3 is designed to open and strengthen ones third eye so you can experience a higher state of consciousness. Simply visit the link below the image to get started.

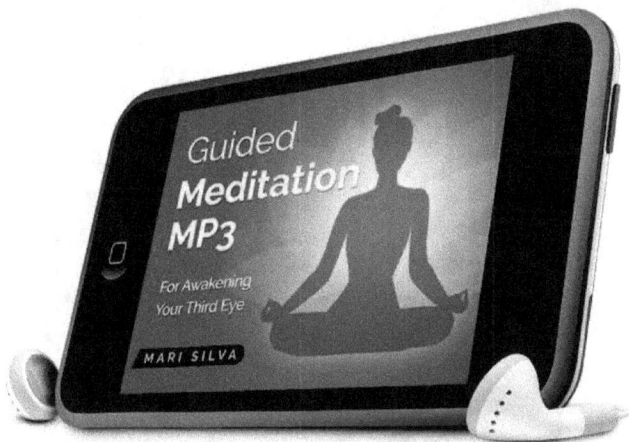

https://spiritualityspot.com/meditation

References

geomancy | method of divination. (n.d.). In Encyclopedia Britannica.

Geomancy - fortune-telling. (n.d.). Magizzle.Com.
https://www.magizzle.com/geomancy/

Painter, S. (n.d.). Geomancy in Feng Shui for beginners. LoveToKnow.
https://feng-shui.lovetoknow.com/feng-shui-tips/geomancy-feng-shui-beginners

(N.d.-a). Princeton.Edu.
https://www.princeton.edu/~ezb/geomancy/geostep.html

(N.d.-b). Princeton.Edu.
https://www.princeton.edu/~ezb/geomancy/geostep.html#:~:text=The%20astrological%20method%20(which%20is,the%20use%20of%20an%20astrolabe.

(N.d.-c). Psychicscience.Org. https://psychicscience.org/geomancy